If you're interested in learning to write books, chances are high that you've tried before and gotten stuck. As a result, you may be even less enthusiastic about trying again. If that's the case, check out some personally selected writing exercises from author Lauren Bingham's vault of helpful tricks and tips for getting the cursor moving again... or for the first time.

Go to

to download your own copy of Lauren Bingham's Five Favorite Writing Exercises.

REVIEWS

Reviews and feedback help improve this book and the author. If you enjoy this book, we would greatly appreciate it if you could take a few moments to share your opinion and post a review on Amazon.

HOW TO WRITE A BOOK

A Book for Anyone Who Has Never Written a Book (But Wants To)

Lauren Bingham

How to Write a Book: A Book for Anyone Who Has Never Written a Book (But Wants To)

One Word at a Time: How to Write a Fiction Book for Beginners

Introduction

"... And that's how Uncle Lester became known as 'The Amazing Flying Parcheezi!'" You finish your story with a flourish as the crowd that has slowly gathered around you gasps and giggles admiringly, while their smattering of applause slowly fades.

"That was a great story!" someone says.

"Your stories are always so good," another person intones. "You should write a book!"

You blush a little, embarrassed that your off-handed story about your off-the-wall uncle had garnered this much attention. "Well, maybe someday," you mumble, waving off the lingering celebrity from your moment in the spotlight. "Maybe someday."

Sometimes that's where the dream ends. You wander back to work, continue socializing at a cocktail party, or go back to doing whatever it was you were doing before you had to spin one of your amazing yarns. But sometimes it's not that easy. You begin to let your mind wander further into the unexplored territory of becoming a published author. It starts with a little nudge like "if I wrote a book, what would it be about?" Then, maybe you creep stealthily into "who would the main characters be?" Before you know it, you've got three plot points scoped out and have made several mental notes to yourself to research whether situation A is possible, whether product B was available in 1957, and to call your mother because you can't remember Uncle Lester's middle name.

It happens to all of us. Once upon a time, I was encouraged to write a book. And, well, you see how that turned out. However, I didn't just wake up, type out a manuscript, and go on with my life. It's been a very long and weird journey from "you should totally write a book" to "would you sign my book?"

I believe that one of the most beautiful things about humans is the stories they tell. Storytelling has given us names for the stars in the sky, and continues to inform us of our past. The stories told by our ancestors have built our world, given us clarity in times of need, and have enthralled us as tales from the deepest reaches of the world circulate in written form.

At the same time, there are many who have scoffed or laughed when I've mentioned that I'm a writer. At first, it used to offend me, but now

I have a stock answer that suits me and the purpose quite well: "Do you ever read?"

Reading is fundamental. While some parties argue that the future will be controlled by robots, and learning to read will be as useless as practicing proper handwriting, the fact remains that reading is still at the core of the process through which those robots will be built. Others argue that television and audiobooks will soon make reading obsolete, but again, you can't have television or audiobooks without someone writing a script. Your automatic, self-driving car might recognize the road signs without your input, but someone needs to program the car so that it can do the reading for you. Plus, even the lightest of duties, such as arguing on social media, require at least a moderate grasp of written language. Reading isn't going anywhere anytime soon, and as long as there is reading, writers will have a place in this world.

Therefore, when people indicate that they find writing to be a worthless pursuit, I have to wonder what they're trying to get out of the experience. If your sole purpose in writing is to enjoy the process of committing the words in your brain and the scenarios of your imagination to paper (and/or the screen of some device in modern times), then your efforts will never be in vain. If, instead, your goal is to write a bestseller, get a movie deal, buy yourself a large house, and become extremely popular for your witty Twitter banter, then the chances are very high that your endeavors will be fruitless. Sure, you may be far more talented than the latest bestselling author, but talent gets books written. Politics and marketing is what turns them into bestsellers.

If you want to write a book, then write a book. Write a book because you need to write a book. Write a book because you're sick of telling the same story and you just want to email everyone the file and be done with it. Write a book because you don't want anyone to forget about "The Amazing Flying Parcheezi". Passion is what makes a project so enjoyable. And if you make any money out of it, so much the better!

Nearly everyone is compelled at some point in their life to turn a thought into a story, a story into a book, and a book into a series. Whether it's a memoir, capturing an oral tale in written format, or weaving a new universe full of fascinating inhabitants who do interesting things, all of us have stories inside us, just bursting to come out. Writing is what gives us the ability to capture all of these things and draw them out into the open from the deep parts of our brain in which they dwell. How can any of us possibly be unworthy of jotting down our thoughts?

That being said, it's only fair to warn you that writing isn't always easy, and it isn't always fun. There are times when you've stared at a blank page without progress for so long that you'll start to wonder if you're still literate. You'll stay up all night and get up before the sun rises because you have to "work out this part here." Your writing will interfere with your life, and your life will dramatically cramp your writing style. But if you want to write, then do it!

This is not a book about how to write a bestseller. This is not about my journey to the top of the *New York Times* list because I haven't gone there, nor do I think I'll ever make that particular trek. The quality of the book you write is entirely up to you. As the saying goes, I make no promises, but I'll tell no lies.

Instead, this book is going to be about the writing process. This tool is intended for anyone who is stuck on the teeter-totter of "should I or shouldn't I" when it comes to writing a book. Instead of talking about things like grammar and kerning, we'll be exploring the work that needs to be completed before you even name your manuscript file. We'll skip the helpful tips for writing a marketable plot, but we'll look at staying organized and focused while your tale comes to life. Rather than going through the steps of finding an agent and shopping for a publisher, we'll comfort and calm those going through the editing process for the first time. Fiction or nonfiction, prose or poetry, there's a little bit of something for everyone when it comes to keeping brains happy and spirits high when attempting to crank out your very first literary attempt.

Whether or not this book convinces you to write your own, you will put it down with confident understanding of what it takes emotionally, physically, and intellectually to write your very first book. While I believe that everyone has a story to tell and platform on which to tell it, only you can decide whether you have the internal fortitude to get through the process.

There's no judgment, either. If this book teaches you that you are not in a place to write a book this very second, then it's done its job. But, if you find yourself taking notes, brainstorming in a secret notebook, or daydreaming your way through significant moments that would be in your book, then maybe it's time to dip a toe or two into the world of writing.

Honestly, the worst thing that could possibly happen is that you never write a book, and that's pretty much how things stand today, isn't it? Perhaps this book is a step towards your new super-stardom as a bestselling author. On the other hand, it could be a precious reminder of why you stick to blogging when you need to exercise your writing chops. Regardless, you're taking a very big step by getting off of that teeter-totter and finding out what it would take to get the job done.

Why Write a Book?

Answering a question with another question is known as "maieutics." In this day and age, it's considered rude, though in Socratic philosophy, it's a necessity. After all, how can we reveal a question's true nature until we have questioned the very question itself? But when you ask yourself why you should write a book, the answer truly is another question: "Why not?"

For many, the process is strange and scary. In fact, even for those of us who have done it a few times, the process remains strange and scary. What if you run out of words? What if you run out of things to talk about? How much time does it take? Am I going to become a recluse? All of these are valid questions, even the "recluse" question. Writing a book can be a very lengthy and passionate undertaking.

There are three main qualities required of those who endeavor to write a book:

1. Time
2. Energy
3. A good sense of humor

Many experts on the topic will say that you need to have an intriguing, solid plot, relatable characters, and a unique writing style to create worthwhile fiction. Meanwhile, nonfiction writers are deemed good at their art if they write academically and stick to solid facts.

My counter-argument is that while those are very good points, first, you must have a book. The most inspirational characters will fail to change lives with their story, and the most accurate factual book in the world will never inform a soul if the author lacks the time, energy, and good humor to get through the writing process. In my opinion, the worst book in the world is the one no one has written.

So how much time does a book take to write? There's really no set answer to that question. One aspiring author may tackle a topic in segments, researching as they go, and taking their time to flesh out each skeletal section deliberately. On the other hand, there are writers who have been sitting on a delicious perspective for so long that they can easily type it out in a matter of days, pausing only for meals, bathroom breaks, and to double-check their facts.

Of course, you may have gotten yourself into a situation in which you need to write a book in time to meet a specific deadline. This can be both a blessing and a curse, as you will be forced to trudge along in order to submit the required assignment, but you may be stressed about keeping yourself on track and focusing on the topic at hand. There is a certain amount of finesse which is required to set and meet deadlines, and we'll take a look at what it takes to remain cool, calm, and collected in the face of the clock in another section.

If you are writing a book because you want to write a book, and not because anyone is expecting you to do so, then you can plan on it taking as long as it takes. But perhaps, at least for your first effort, you should give yourself a few milestones to complete in order to keep the process marching along. That could mean deciding where you want to begin and end your book, creating a hypothesis that must be proven, or simply choosing a page number and the date you hope to have that many pages written by.

Most writers can produce a few thousand words per writing session, but they also do a lot of work before, during, and after the writing process itself. The amount of research that can go into a book is absolutely staggering. You might think that fiction lends itself to less factual integrity, but you'll still find it's important to find out if your characters can reasonably be behind the wheel of that specific vehicle given the context of the story, or to find the right descriptive words for the architecture of the setting you're trying to portray. After all, there's a distinct difference between "Generations of ivy grew unchecked on the facade of the old bungalow, which seemed to crumble before our very eyes" and "Generations of ivy grew unchecked on the glass walls of the skyscraper, giving it a surprisingly cozy ambience."

Therefore, when you consider the amount of time you're willing to spend on a book, bear in mind that not every moment is going to result in a productive keystroke. You'll backspace, delete, undo, copy, paste, stare into the abyss and wonder what you've done, and go back to the drawing board several times. We'll talk about this process in more detail later as well. But for now, the answer to the eternal question "How long does it take to write a book?" can either be answered with "a month" or "your entire lifetime."

In order to manage all of this time, you must have energy as well. Sitting in a chair while typing for hours at a time can cause all sorts of pain: neck and back pain from sitting for so long, wrist anguish from the unnatural position we assume to type, and infinite headaches from endlessly staring at a screen. But none of these physical ailments compare to the mental strain of attempting to write a book.

According to many writers-- and as actively reinforced by professors, teachers, and many websites on the matter-- you should be able to log 2,000 words a day in order to be considered an "effective" or "productive" writer. National Novel Writing Month, or NaNoWriMo as it's affectionately known, also encourages writers to exercise their mind and spirit by coughing up at least 2,000 words each day. Truly, this is an admirable number to aspire to, and setting goals is extremely important, as we'll discuss shortly. But there will be days where, as a human with other things to do in your life besides anguish and toil over a simple tome, you might as well wring blood from a stone as write something coherent, let alone meaningful.

Some may call this affliction "writer's block." I call it what it really is: running out of energy. Mental, physical, emotional, spiritual... Any deficit in these categories will lead to the brain and hands stubbornly refusing to produce words on a page. And to add insult to injury, you can't just force your way through it like a profusely bleeding soldier marching stolidly onward through the blasts of fuselage and relent- less terror. There are things you can do to redirect what energy you have and possibly conjure up a little inspiration. Every professional writer has their own arsenal of tricks to fool the brain into believing any time is a good time to write, but this is your first book. This isn't your life's devotion (yet). You aren't getting paid (yet). You're just a regular person, writing a single book (so you think) which you'll never do again (so you say). You don't need to know all the professional tips and tricks if you're not going to be a professional, but they can offer you some assistance when you inevitably run out of energy. Should you decide you do need those tips and tricks, you'll find them in the "Resources" section at the end of this book.

As for the last prescription, "a good sense of humor," it should seem pretty logical that the act of writing a book is intensely illogical. Whether you're using a typewriter, laptop, quill, or ball point pen, there's nothing simple or straightforward about writing a book. It is simply a necessary activity to which many of us are drawn.

If you don't meet that 2,000 word quota, you need to have the good cheer to simply move on and recognize that Scarlett O'Hara (via Margaret Mitchell) had it right when she said, "Tomorrow is another day." One day might be a 6,000 word day. The next day might yield a mere 6 words. If you overwhelm yourself with the seriousness of being "behind schedule," you'll find yourself creating stress. Stress is best known for its ability to sap all of your available energy. No energy, as we've established, means no book. Don't allow yourself to become stressed.

That's not to say it's important to remain cheerful and delightful every step of the way. The archetype of the artist or creator states that we must be moody, choleric, woeful, and always in the throes of romantically piteous agony. My personal suggestion is that you be-have as you would normally behave. Just allow yourself a mote of forgiveness if things aren't coming out the way you'd like.

In fact, for your first effort, I recommend not holding yourself to any sort of expectations. Set milestones, but don't actually carve them into stone. Instead of 2,000 words a day, consider, "I'll have gotten through Uncle Lester's childhood years by the end of the month." This way, you have a goal in mind to keep you marching, but it isn't measured by letters, words, or hours spent scratching away at your masterpiece. Instead, you can keep track of your progress by your involvement in developing the tale you intend to tell. Making milestones manageable is just one way to keep a sense of humor while you're writing your first opus.

I also strongly recommend that you hold back any urge to edit as you write. Of course you can backspace or scratch out any misspellings, and if you look at the phrase you've just written and immediately think of a better way to write it, then by all means do so. But if you spend every day agonizing over the past 2,000 words, you'll never find the next 2,000 words. Some writers call these "sprints," in which they create a finish line for the day, and then simply write, write, write until they reach the finish line. Don't look back; just keep putting one word after another. There will be plenty of time to edit once you've got a full book. In fact, a sentence that looks like utter garbage today might become absolute poetry once you've filled in the paragraphs following it. Provide yourself enough grace to not micromanage yourself until you've completed the task at hand.

And lastly, on the "sense of humor" topic, I want to urge you to remember that once you have birthed your opus into the world, it will no longer belong to you. Of course, it's your original material. All of the thoughts contained are your own, and any likeness or resemblance is purely coincidental, etc., but it is no longer just your baby. Your baby is going to be read by anyone who gets their hands on it, and it's not going to mean to them what it means to you.

That is to say, once the thoughts are out of your head and on paper (or screen, depending on your format of choice), those who consume said thoughts are going to interpret them in their own way. Someone with different thoughts, opinions, experiences, and understandings is going to look at your work and critique it based on what they know.

With any luck, your published book will attract the right kind of reader. This is where intelligent marketing comes in, which we'll certainly touch on later in this book. But inevitably, your book will wander into the hands of someone who just doesn't get it. This person will read what they can, and immediately take to the internet to let everyone know that they found your book to be a wad of mindless drivel that is best used to prop up wonky furniture. Not everyone will love you or appreciate your efforts. Remember that it's not personal; it's just an internet review.

One of my first books earned a review that said something to the effect of "everything in this book can be found on the internet." It was a "how-to" book. My first reaction was of shock and horror. I thought I'd completely failed. Then, I really thought about it. The person who wrote that comment wasn't wrong-- everything in the book really could have been found on the internet. But when you think about it, that's exactly how the internet works. If you're doing it right, you should be able to verify every factoid in a "how-to" book via the internet. I'd be more concerned if you couldn't double-check the author's work in a nonfiction scenario because if the author made it all up, then it's fiction, right?

Regardless of semantics and critiques, allow yourself to brush off the harsh comments. Allow yourself to have patience and kindness with yourself throughout the process, from the pre-work to the reviews and beyond. Acknowledge that this is not going to be easy, but accept reassurance from those who have been there before that it is fully rewarding. Be prepared to ride a Tilt-A-Whirl of emotions, and learn when to provide yourself a little grace.

If you don't, I assure you that you will learn all of these things throughout the process of creating your first book. But it's a lot easier if you get yourself into a good headspace before you even commit the first word to file.

Before You Start Writing

Before you start writing a book, you should know what type of book you want to write. In many cases, that's much easier said than done. There are some books that lend themselves fantastically to a particular genre or format; for example, "How to Write a Book" is obviously going to be a nonfiction book. I could make the whole thing up, but it's much easier to tell the truth than to reinvent the entire process. Besides, who on Earth would make up a mess like this? But for many authors, you have to decide what to do with your concept before you can go any further.

I encourage aspiring writers to do as much daydreaming at this stage as possible. Obviously, you'll want to tone it down when you're doing treacherous things that require the utmost concentration, such as driving a forklift through a crowded warehouse or guiding a Conestoga wagon over rocky mountain passes. But there are plenty of times when we can put down the phone, tablet, or whatever you use to occupy your mind when it's not in use and do a little constructive daydreaming. This is how you figure out what your book is really about.

When we think about writing a book, we tend to get all tense and serious about it. Instead, approach thinking about a book the same way you think about what you're getting for lunch when you're driving into the office at 7:30am. Dream about it. Make wishlists. Explore different avenues. Think about words you want to use. Throw around some concepts you'd like to introduce and how they'd work together. Words are like Tinker Toys, Legos, Lincoln Logs, or whatever building toy you like to use in analogies-- they fit together in many different ways, so play with them to figure out how you want to use them. Keep your efforts loose and natural so they don't sound forced, stressed, or anxious when you finally write them all down.

If you're the type who likes chaos, then you'll keep all of this pre-work in your head. If you like to proceed about life in a nice and orderly sort of way, then you might want to have a journal or jot pad for this. I personally find notes stressful. If I can't live up to my notes, then I feel like I've failed. Therefore, the only written evidence you'll find of my pre-work is my research and my proposed table of contents (TOC). In fact, my proposed TOCs rarely look like my final product, so I'm not even sure they can be forensically linked to each other.

As odd as it may seem, it may take you a few days or daydreams to figure out the simple question of, "What is my book going to be?" In fact, you might consider this your first challenge as an author: to free yourself from your own expectations and write a book that genuinely reflects the message you want to relay to the public.

If you want to write the story of The Amazing Flying Parcheezi, Uncle Lester, then what's the best way to do it? Should you go for a facts-only family memoir style with interviews from the legend himself? Should you write it in the format of third-person short stories with a little artistic license taken to give the tales a vivid, life-like quality? You could go dark and mysterious, employing the second person perspective to engage and immerse the reader in the experience. You can include local colloquialisms to drive home the cozy, family setting. You can paint a full picture with lavish descriptions, or you can allow the reader to play with your characters in their own setting by leaving all of the details to the imagination with minimal word play. There are so many choices, and they all belong to you.

In the next chapters, we'll look at how to get organized before writing. The first chapter is for those who are ready to walk on the wild side of fiction, while the second chapter is for those who want to stick with the weird things we already know about the nonfiction format. Allow me to ruin your misconceptions by informing you that neither is easier than the other, and all writers are deeply challenged by the books they choose to write. Regardless, here are some solid points of advice to help you get organized before you start writing.

Chapter 1: For Aspiring Fiction Writers

I have nothing but admiration for fiction writers. I have written my fair share of fiction, and I've enjoyed the process, but I always feel a bit self-conscious when I'm done. I end up questioning and dragging myself through a rabbit hole of "what ifs." "What if Character A had made a different decision in Chapter 4?" "Does Character B's dialogue make them sound like a giant jerk during the big scene in Chapter 10?" "Do we even need Character C?" "Why did I concentrate so much on describing this thing when I hardly even mentioned that other thing?" Fiction is not for the faint of heart or those who have difficulty making decisions. At least, not without a sympathetic editor.

Fiction writing is storytelling without limits. Your story can take place anywhere, at any time, with a cast of any characters you can imagine. Want to drop off one of today's billionaire playboys in feudal Europe of the 1500s? Do it. Need your characters to head out to space for an important plot point? Have them build a rocket out of car parts. As long as you write it, your readers will follow along.

This is where the notion of genres comes in. According to the Merriam-Webster Dictionary, a genre is: *a category of artistic, musical, or literary composition characterized by a particular style, form, or content.* Science fiction, romance, fantasy, myth, mystery, horror, and historical fiction are just a handful of examples of different genres. Some stories blend a few different aspects of standard genres; Neil Gaiman's *American Gods* is a highly regarded example of genre bending.

The very fascinating thing about all genres is that each one takes the world as we know it and completely reinvents it. Take, for example, the *Harry Potter* series. While the story takes place in modern day England, as we know it, the entire wizarding society complete with cultural mores, language, and biological traits has been invented by author J.K. Rowling. There's enough reality for us to understand the character traits, emotions, and actions of her characters, but the fantasy world is completely from the author's own mind.

Does that mean you have to invent an entire world just to write a good fiction book? Not necessarily, but you have to conjure up enough of a world so that your tale has a place where it can reasonably occur. Even though your fictional world may not be tangible, as an author, you know exactly where Main Street and First Avenue intersect. You know what everyone drives and where they eat dinner. They get their groceries from one of three supermarkets, though there is a farmer's market in the summer. The snooty people are from one neighborhood, and the "across the tracks" area is marked by a specific geographic location.

So, what happens if you aren't using a time or place that you're as familiar with? Well, you start researching and learning what you need to know in order to create a place of your own. But we're getting just a little bit ahead of ourselves here. For now, we'll settle the debate of "what is fiction?" with "a tale that comes entirely from your imagination, generally subscribing to one or more literary genres."

What does it take to write a spectacular work of fiction that everyone will want to read? You'll need that world that we just talked about-- and shall continue to talk about in greater specifics. You'll need to introduce characters that readers will care about. Those characters will need to be involved in some great conflict which builds throughout the tale before reaching a climactic turning point. Then, there is some form of resolution or denouement in which all of the dangling threads of your tale are brought to a conclusion.

Sounds really simple, doesn't it? Except if you were to write a story that was as simple as that description, it would be a sentence. "Bill, a good-looking fellow in his early 30s, awoke one morning and nearly fell down the stairs; however, he caught his balance by grabbing onto the railing and continued out the door to his unsatisfactory retail job." By definition, that is a full story, but it's probably not going to sell millions of copies, and the movie would be incredibly short.

Therefore, a good fiction story needs to have more purpose to it than that. This is where the work comes in and when many people abandon the idea of writing a book in the first place. There are an awful lot of little hazy details that need to be figured out before you start writing, otherwise you end up with stream-of-consciousness drivel… unless that's what you were going for in the first place, with all due respect to William Faulkner.

To begin your work of fiction, you will need a character map and a plot outline. Some seasoned writers recommend starting with the characters, while others recommend starting with the plot. Both, in my opinion, are incredibly important, so I find it difficult to ignore one in favor of the other. However, both will need to be outlined, and unless you have the astounding skill of being able to write two different things with each hand simultaneously, you'll need to handle them one at a time.

The Character Map

The character map can be a literal map, as the name implies, or an Excel spreadsheet, or a very organized list. You can use pictures to help visualize your characters or jot down the details of their appearance. The point of a character map is to bring out all of the potential characters in your tale, establish who they are and how they're connected to each other, and decide the roles they play within your story. There are plenty of templates of character maps available online, some of which I've linked at the end of this book; however, you also have the option to free-form list this information in a way that makes sense to you.

That last bit-- "in a way that makes sense to you"-- is really crucial for the pre-work. Your notes need to be thorough enough so that you can glance at them and know exactly what you meant. This can be somewhat difficult if your characters summon you from a deep sleep or while you're changing lanes on a major freeway, but be as detailed as it's safe and sane to be when making your notes. There is nothing quite as frustrating as looking at your notes to see something vague like "don't forget Elizabeth's hair" only to realize you have not only forgotten Elizabeth's hair, but who Elizabeth is in the first place. Instead, something like, "Elizabeth, Penn's sister, is always brushing her hair, which is why Penn is implicated at the crime scene when a long blonde hair is discovered on the body," will better serve you to keep everyone and everything organized.

So who are your characters? Who do you include on your map? Your protagonist, of course, or the hero of your tale. The term "hero" does not mean they have to behave like Superman or Captain America. Instead, this indicates that it is the actions to and of this person, along with their reactions, that will help develop the plot of this tale. There can be more than one protagonist, although generally speaking, only one steps into the lead role. For example, there are plenty of wizards and witches who keep things moving along in the *Harry Potter* series, but there's also a reason it's not called the *Harry Potter and Friends* series. Young Harry is written into a role that requires some heavy lifting, emotionally speaking, so he is the main protagonist.

Then, you've got the antagonist. Traditionally speaking, we think of the antagonist as the "bad guy" or the "villain." This is a bit of a misnomer because the antagonist isn't obligated to be morally evil; instead, this character opposes the protagonist. They help generate and perpetuate the conflict at the center of the story. Romeo and Juliet's parents, for example, aren't inherently evil. They just happen to be participants in a long-standing strife. It's technically the familial feud-- and their participation therein-- that causes the tragic end to the star-crossed lovers' lives. But they are still considered the antagonists of their tale.

Therefore, when you're dreaming up your characters, think less in terms of "good guy/bad guy," and more in terms of "people perpetuating conflicting opinions." It's your choice from there to emphasize the morality or evil of their roles.

Then, there are supporting characters. Supporting characters often get a reputation as being afterthoughts or leftovers, but they're actually the main reason the plot moves along in the first place. You could write a novel in which the protagonist and antagonist only interact with each other. However, from the standpoint of the reader, it's often helpful to have additional characters around to keep the story moving forward. In *The Girl Who Loved Tom Gordon* by Stephen King, a large portion of the story follows a little girl wandering alone in the woods, yet we know that she has a family waiting for her. Her hopes of being reunited with her family-- the supporting characters-- are what drive the plot forward while she wanders.

Supporting characters do all sorts of wonderful things. They can demonstrate the social norms. They can be sounding boards for the protagonist and antagonist. They can be the voice of reason or the devil's advocate. They can show the readers the truth that the protagonist and antagonist can't see because they're too wrapped up in their own worlds. They can be friends, family, housemates, love interests, or people who have managed to walk into the same shop at the same time as one of the main characters.

So, how many characters is the right number of characters? That depends substantially on what you're using them for. A traditional Greek chorus includes up to 50 performers, but there's no particular requirement. As the author, it is your prerogative to give every citizen in town a voice or to simplify your story by limiting the number of speakers with backstories.

There are a few things to keep in mind when it comes to choosing your roster of characters, and the map you create can help you organize these tenets of character building. First, there's a difference between full-blown characters and people who happen to show up in your story. For example, if you have a scene taking place at a grocery store, the elderly lady who asks for assistance in putting a watermelon in her cart for the sole purpose of interrupting your protagonist's train of thought doesn't necessarily have to be a complete character. Ask yourself if it makes sense to give her a name, backstory, full purpose in the plot, relationship to the protagonist, and a specific role in the overall quest. She can, but that's up to you and how much time you want to spend detailing all of this information to readers if she's never going to appear again.

Next, consider what a potential character will provide to the overall plot. If, for example, you decide to write in the very popular trope of a love triangle, make sure it has something to do with the story. If Matt is trying to decide whether he loves Rebecca or Renee, and the reader never actually meets Renee, then why do we even care about her? What purpose does she have to the story? Unless you very clearly indicate how Matt's resilient passion for the mysterious and unseen force of Renee is impeding his ability to behave appropriately, clouding his judgement or causing him to do cruel things to Rebecca, for example, then it's really not important for the reader to know very much about Renee.

Furthermore, you don't need to write an entire dossier on each person who steps into the book. That may seem like a direct conflict to the "make the characters count" advice, but it's actually part of the same tip. Try to think of your characters as friends you are introducing to your reader. You aren't going to share every intimate detail you know about them, such as their favorite color is orange, their favorite drink is a gin tonic, and the last time they got a haircut was in February, unless all of those details are important to the future relationship between the character and the reader. In the moment that Maya is hanging from the side of a helicopter with a machete, flying towards a burning building, we don't need to know that she was born in a small town in Oklahoma, loves green beans, and once had a pet duck named Pyjamas. It would be helpful, however, to know that she spent four years training with a Russian gymnastics team as part of her undercover role with the CIA, but how you choose to reveal that information to the reader is up to you as the author.

Lastly, it's always a good idea to give each character an entrance, duty, and exit, especially if they do something significant within the plot. That doesn't mean we have to follow them around every day through the entire story, but even the elderly woman at the grocery store can wheel her cart up to the protagonist, ask for assistance, and then dutifully disappear into the "Cereal and Breakfast Foods" aisle. Having someone appear, do something very important, leave a lasting impression in the readers' minds, and then just vanish like they never existed can be very distracting and confusing to readers. They can walk away, get in their car and drive off, go home, or get Raptured during the climax of your story, just as long as it makes sense within the context of the story for them to stop appearing.

As you can see, there's a lot to organize when it comes to creating characters which is what makes the concept of a character map so very handy. You can see who is who, when they enter and leave the story, what they contribute to the plot, and what we need to know about them in order to understand their role. Some very talented writers can do all of this without making notes. I am not one of them. Therefore, I always recommend those trying out this whole "writing thing" for the first time to at least start with a character map. If you turn out to be naturally organized and prepared in the face of chaos, then you haven't done anything to hinder the process, and if it just so happens that you need a little help with the organization process, then you're already set up for success!

The Plot Outline

Alongside the character map, you'll need to create a plot outline. A plot outline allows you to map out how you're going to get from Point A, meaning the first page of your story, to Point B when the first part of the rising action occurs, to Point C and so on until you've reached the natural conclusion of your tale.

Before your head starts whirling at the idea of having bitten off more than you can chew, let's step back a moment to look at what constitutes a plot:

1. Exposition or introduction
2. Rising action
3. Climax or turning point
4. Falling action
5. Resolution or denouement

The exposition or introduction is just that. This section of your story establishes where we are, who the characters are, and in a sense, why we care. One of my favorite examples of a very neat and tidy exposition is the Prologue to William Shakespeare's *Romeo and Juliet*:

> *"Two households, both alike in dignity,*
> *In fair Verona, where we lay our scene,*
> *From ancient grudge break to new mutiny,*
> *Where civil blood makes civil hands unclean.*
> *From forth the fatal loins of these two foes*
> *A pair of star-cross'd lovers take their life;*
> *Whose misadventured piteous overthrows*
> *Do with their death bury their parents' strife.*
> *The fearful passage of their death-mark'd love,*
> *And the continuance of their parents' rage,*

Which, but their children's end, nought could remove,

Is now the two hours' traffic of our stage;

The which if you with patient ears attend,

What here shall miss, our toil shall strive to mend."

Everything you need to know before the characters take the stage is laid out here. The location is Verona, Italy. We're about to meet two well-to-do families, and their children are going to fall in love. Sadly, it's not going to end well. Shakespeare even does us the favor of letting us know the whole thing should take about two hours to get through.

Your introduction doesn't have to be in iambic pentameter, of course; prose is fine. You also don't have to feel the need to be as quick about it. Depending on the length of your book and the story you're going to tell, you can spend pages upon pages and entire chapters on building towards the point of your story, as long as everything you say is important to the journey.

Deciding what's important to the journey is the whole point of the plot outline in the first place. Sure, you can just open a Word document and wing it, but you're going to need to keep track of where all of your characters are at all times, what subplots are unfolding and why, and most of all, you'll need to figure out why your audience cares about all this. Sure, it's fun to write a whole bunch of intimate and outlandish details, but does your intended reader want to read all of it?

Take, for example, Bram Stoker's description of the setting in Chapter 16 of *Dracula*:

"Never did tombs look so ghastly white. Never did cypress, or yew, or juniper so seem the embodiment of funeral gloom. Never did tree or grass wave or rustle so ominously. Never did bough creak so mysteriously, and never did the far-away howling of dogs send such a woeful presage through the night."

While it's true that Stoker used a lot of words here to establish the fact that it was really creepy outside, he did so for a reason. He's setting the scene with words and phrases that would be meaningful to his intended audience. There was no television or radio at the time. People of his era had a limited understanding of the world around them, bolstered by occasional travel and getting their hands on books such as *Dracula*. These words would have chilled them to the very bone, while readers today might read these words thinking, "Yes, yes, it's creepy- just get on with it!"

Therefore, when creating your introduction to your tale, think of what your readers want or need to know about the world they are preparing to enter, and hook them in by writing to them in the same tone that you would tell this story if you were speaking out loud. While you should never write a book for anyone but yourself, you should communicate in words that emphasize the message you are delivering.

Once you've made a sufficient introduction, it's time to start weaving in the rising action. One common first time misconception is that the introduction/exposition and the rising action can't happen at the same time. There is no particular formula that states that pages 1-32 should be exclusively expository and the rising action should begin promptly on page 33. Consider how many different types of literature there are, how many genres and styles make up the literary world, and how the very act of telling a story can change shape even as the story unfolds. *Dracula,* for example, is told through letters and diary entries. The *Harry Potter* series is told in third person narrative. Both of them deal with interweaving the rising action in different ways.

If you recall from earlier, I mentioned that reading is fundamental, and this is why. In order to write a book, you must understand books. I'm not suggesting you copy any one author, or completely adopt a tone that's entirely unlike your own, or do anything that might skitter into the world of plagiarism. Instead, I'm asking that you read a lot so you can get a feel for how books work. The more you read, the more options you have for understanding how your own book works.

Take, for example, two of the books mentioned so far: The rising action in *Dracula* takes place slowly, in tiny steps, to thoroughly invest and creep out the reader. The rising action in *Harry Potter and the Sorcerer's Stone* takes place all at once when a door bursts open and Hagrid steps in to disrupt everything. The swirling, whirling mayhem that ensues reflects and emphasizes Harry's confusion at this whole new world unfurling before him.

So, let's look back at your plot outline so far. You've got notes on what needs to be covered in the exposition, and then what you hope to achieve in the rising action, and you're not entirely sure how you're going to do that. Some writers like to flesh things out as they create their plot outline. Others-- myself included-- like to get the whole skeleton out before they start adding limbs.

That brings us to the climax, or turning point. This is the point of no return. All of the conflict in your tale so far has brought us to this moment: the final battle, the face-off, the big decision, the crowning moment. It is very easy to shirk away from a big climactic scene. In fact, all throughout my scholastic career, I got marks for "not making enough conflict." Your story doesn't have to have a great big bang, but it does need to make the reader feel and understand the difference from "before" aka- the world revealed in the exposition, versus "now," or the way things will be after the climax.

Stephen King does glorious battle scenes that really reflect how we deal with our demons, both internal and external. Harry Potter whips out the wand. Romeo and Juliet end their lives in a tomb. Every story has some major event where the main character realizes they can't continue doing things the way they did before, and they make a very important change. Some just do it with magic and poison.

Once you've decided what the climax is going to be, you might suddenly think about all the things that you can include in the rising action to help you get to that point. Write all of those things down, even if they're in conflict with each other and can't possibly make sense if all used at once. Your plot outline is about possibilities and potential; you'll make the tough decisions later.

From the climax, you then have to figure out a way back down. Generally speaking, the laws of gravity apply to literature as well as anything else, and the falling action takes far less time than the rising action. Basically, now that you've gone in and shaken everything up by having your protagonist face strife and struggle, you've had the climax, and now it's time to clean everything up.

Long ago, a writing professor told us something very important and logical, which, in our quest for belonging among the literary elite, we had forgotten: The purpose of the falling action isn't to make everything tidy and digestible for the reader. Instead, it is intended to demonstrate how things are different. You spent the introduction painting a portrait of life in the "before times." You spent countless pages building up the drama and tension to demonstrate how change was going to be difficult, then you've got the climax in which your protagonist is forced to make some sort of major change. Now the reader needs to know what's different and why.

This falling action leads to the resolution or denouement. This is where you wrap things up for this particular tale. This does not, however, have to be the so-called "end" of things. If you have a sequel or series in mind, you might want to make sure you keep enough metaphorical doors and windows open to allow for the next tale. Another option is the oft-complained-about ambiguous ending, wherein we don't know if everyone went home and had a wonderful day, if more conflict arose, or if the world in which your characters live simply blinked out of existence. The purpose of the end of the book isn't necessarily to make things all pat and neat, but to provide a finishing point for the story you are telling. While in theory, you could continue writing forever and ever, that's simply not how books currently work.

Ending your book can be very difficult for a variety of reasons. It can be emotional, since you've spent hours, days, and months leading up to this point. You might have a hard time figuring out how to get the ending just right so that you've tied up all the loose ends without rushing or over-explaining things. Stay calm. Don't panic. Write what feels... right. Take a break. Read what you just wrote. Take another break to think it over. Make notes. Revisit and tinker. I personally recommend saving each version of your ending, if you don't use a program that already stores a version history. Don't throw your scribbles into the fire or trash bin until you're absolutely certain you'll never visit them again.

As we wrap up this section on building a plot, I'll share something that is surprisingly not mentioned often in the writing community: All of these things can change. Your first version of your plot outline and the book that you actually write may be significantly different. You might start writing according to plan and realize that your antagonist would never do that thing, or your protagonist wouldn't care about a particular situation. It is completely natural to discover new and exciting things about your characters and your story as you're writing it.

More importantly, it's important that you quell any negative reaction you might have to these changes. Let it happen. Write it through. Explore where things are going. If it ends up being totally out of scope or making you unhappy, go back to where you feel things took a wrong turn and go another direction. Don't stifle your creative flow just because you thought things would go a very specific way. You might just find-- as many before you have-- that you have more than one story you'd like to tell!

And finally, fear not if you have a lot of questions about the actual writing process after reading this-- we'll get further into those specifics shortly.

Making It All "Real"

So now that you've got all the prospective characters semi fleshed-out, and you've created a basic outline for what you plan on writing, you've got just two chores left:

1. Write a book
2. Make it good

Super simple, right? This is the part where you might feel equal parts prepared and terrified. This is normal. In fact, that feeling is going to be pretty normal from here on out. Regardless, this is when things start to feel "real." And as a prospective author, it's your job to really make it "real."

So, how does an author make a completely fake, invented, imagined, and fully contrived world feel "real" to the reader? Research, obtaining resources, and even conducting interviews.

You might be actively objecting as you read these words. "I'm inventing an entire world! I don't need to do research!" I'm terribly sorry to burst your bubble, but everyone needs to do research. Everything you imagine is based, in some part, on what we recognize and understand in this reality. The time it takes your characters to travel from one imagined location to the next city is going to be based on your understanding of distances and the speed of travel as we know it, even if they use a mode of transportation specifically invented by you at this exact moment. From the type of dwelling they live in, to the color of their planet, to the distance to the nearest star, you're going to need at least a sliver of reality on which to base your imagination. And you know what makes for good imagination? Thorough research.

That's not to say that everything in your story has to be absolutely accurate. Readers will forgive a cheat here and there, if they even notice at all. But when you're describing people, places, situations, animals, even the food on the table, it helps if you have a clear mental picture of what you're describing. Mental pictures are formed by experiencing a lot of different people, places, situations, animals, and so on. Therefore, taking the time to research these points will help you gain a broader view of the possibilities which can help you describe them in rich detail. The reward is that the reader will climb on board without question.

The suspension of disbelief is necessary for fiction to work at all. The more detailed your descriptions, the more accurate your tour of your new world, and the more "real" everything feels, even if it's not real at all, the more willing your readers will be to drop any preconceived notions and come along for the ride.

Resources can come in many different packages. If you're trying to truly capture the essence of an experience, whether that's traveling cross-country, climbing a mountain, shooting into space, or whatever you fancy, it's a great idea to hear from those who have actually done those things. Blogs, vlogs, and social media groups for those who have an interest in those activities can really help you gain insight into what people appreciate and detest about those activities. When you write about it like it's real, it becomes real. Therefore, take your time to see what that lifestyle entails.

You may wish to conduct interviews, either in person, or via phone or email/direct message/etc, with those who have expertise regarding the things you're writing about. Right now, that may seem like overkill for a fiction book, but it can be incredibly rewarding to get some different perspectives about a particular activity, lifestyle, scenario, or aspect of your book that you have limited experience or understanding about.

In my own experience, I once contacted a gentleman I met through mutual friends regarding his car. I have driven many cars in my life, but I had not driven a 1971 Buick Riviera. This fellow had a 1973 Riviera. We took it for a spin, and I asked him questions about the maintenance, the steering, the gas mileage, and he even let me push all the buttons. I didn't necessarily use every single detail we discussed, but I felt much more confident about the frequency with which I had my character stop for fuel on his drive, and his radio had the same glitch my new friend's vehicle had. It made for a much more believable scene with confident descriptions, instead of vaguely referencing the automobile and hoping no one would think about it too much.

I could wax on eternally about the benefit of doing substantial research, but to avoid droning on, I'll leave you with this thought: If at any time you find yourself wondering how you could make your book just a little richer, your descriptions a little deeper, and your world just a little more immersive, consider heading to the web or popping open a book to go the extra mile with your research.

At the end of the day, what you actually do before you start writing your novel is up to you. I certainly recommend a character map and a plot outline, and I encourage you to do as much research before you get started as possible, but sometimes that little word, "possible," gets in the way. For some writers, the best way to get started is to just sit down and start typing, fill in the character map along the way, and jot down the plot outline as you start thinking of it, scribbling with one hand while the other attempts to type. I, myself, have once awoken with a story that was burning so brightly, I had no choice but to pull open the laptop at 2am and start typing everything I could think of. That being said, once I reached the point where the brain worm stopped and I was on my own again, you can bet I had my notebook out, writing out everything I knew about the characters and where they were headed.

In the words of one of my mentors, "I don't care how it gets organized, but get some sense in here!" That is to say, if you need to write a bit before you create your map and outline, then do it. I will say, however, that the earlier you start organizing in the process, the easier it will be to continue to stay organized, especially when it comes to little fiddly things, like small but very important characters or subtle plot details that carry all the subtext of your story. Set yourself up for success, not stress.

Chapter 2: Nonfiction, Please; I'm Trying to Cut Back

Nonfiction, as the name implies, is the absence of fiction. These books are based on facts and are used to share information to discuss, educate, and raise questions for debate amongst your audience. Many people think of nonfiction as dry and boring, but it really doesn't have to be. Consider these various genres:

- History

- Biography

- Philosophy

- Religion and spirituality

- Politics

- Scientific research

- Business

- Self-Help

- Travel

- How-To

These are just a few of the subjects included in the realm of nonfiction. Nonfiction books can be informative or educational expository writing, persuasive pieces that prove a point, arguments that attempt to change the readers' minds, descriptive pieces that take readers to an entirely different time or place, or a narrative of a true event, place, or person. Some people feel that nonfiction should not include opinions or use a casual tone, but get a few pages into a Bill Bryson book or guitarist Slash's autobiography, and you'll see that's not always the case.

Nonfiction books can use a variety of different tones to express their content. The tone an author uses is directly dependent on these factors:

- The content

- The audience
- The intention

The content is your book's topic and the angle you choose to explore. A biographical piece in reverence to Pope John Paul II and a biographical account exploring Billy the Kid's role in establishing the economy of the Wild West would have entirely different tones due to the subject matter at hand. Similarly, a book detailing how to fix the mechanical pieces of a Volkswagen Beetle and a book guiding you through daily meditation practices would read differently too.

The audience is also important when choosing the tone of your nonfiction piece. Most people prefer to read books that come across as a conversation with a like-minded friend. If your audience is mostly teenagers, you'll use an entirely different tone than you would writing the business advice of a Fortune 500 CEO.

Lastly, the overall intention of your book will dictate the right voice to use when writing it. The intention is somewhat of a secondary piece to the topic, angle, and audience. Essentially, this is the effect you want your book to have on the people who read it. Do you want them finishing the book with a bit of admiration for Billy the Kid? Do you want them to have enough information to write a basic essay on your book for their science exam? Do you want them to feel like they have a blueprint for the next chapter of their own lives? What you aim to do with your words has a significant impact on how you use them.

So now that you have carved out a bit of headspace for your nonfiction book, it's time to do the pre-work.

Choose a Topic

Choosing the topic of your nonfiction book is possibly the easiest part of the process. Chances are very good that you've had something on your mind lately. Perhaps you've been casually obsessing over a period in history, or you've always been interested in a specific individual who has walked this planet. We all have that "something" that we know a bit more about than the average person.

On the other hand, you may wish to write about something simply because it is unfamiliar, and you want to share your exploration of this new topic with the world, allowing them an intimate look at your learning and growing processes. This is not unheard of, especially in travel books. The journal format is very popular, as it gives others insight into the process and encourages others to do the same.

Your topic may be very broad at first. You might decide to write about pyramids, for example, but that's a vast subject. Which culture? Which continent? Which type of pyramids? You see where this is headed.

You can endeavor to write a book that discusses every pyramid known to date, but you're going to need to consider how you plan to do that. A picture and short blurb of each one? A region-by-region guide with a map and brief history? The possibilities are overwhelming.

Therefore, I recommend you allow yourself some time to really sit and cogitate on your topic. Perhaps you write down the topic you have in mind in the shortest form possible. Then you give it some thought. Run to the library or do a Google search of that topic, using the same term you did when you wrote it down. Let yourself go down the proverbial rabbit hole. Figure out what you love about it. Learn new things about your topic. Not only will this help you narrow down the points you want to make regarding your subject, but it will also inspire greater confidence that you're heading in the right direction.

Perhaps, however, you're starting with a topic that's already pretty niche. You are certainly permitted to take the rabbit hole journey as well; you might discover new facts that you wish to highlight in your book that bolster the discussion you have in mind. Regardless, write down your very well-specified topic and start brainstorming.

From the main topic, you'll want to come up with some of the main points you want to make with your book. If it's a biography, what are the main points of your subject's life that you wish to cover? If it's a self-help book, what are the steps that someone must complete in order to reach the intended outcome? If you're writing a history of a location, what is the timeframe or periods you'd like to highlight? While it would be wonderful if someone would write a book about absolutely everything of all time, that's a bit impractical, especially for your first outing.

Take your time with this. I speak from experience when I say there's nothing as frustrating as starting a nonfiction book and realizing about six pages in that there's really no book there. You may find that you can write a compelling essay, but certainly not an entire book. Or perhaps there simply aren't enough resources to allow you to fully investigate the topic. Experts may have just as many questions about it as you do. Go down as many rabbit holes as you need to. Talk to your friends. Get in arguments about it on social media. Do whatever it takes to really get your topic into focus with enough material to write a complete book upon the matter.

My personal favorite format is the outline. Some people prefer maps, swimlanes, or lists, but I love a good outline. I start by typing out the main topic. Then, I let the main ideas come out. Under each main idea, I then include the points I would like to make about that idea. From the points, I add my evidence, opinions, or supporting facts. The process takes me about a week, because I keep changing it.

Sometimes I'll submit an outline to a publisher with notes describing what I think might change. Sometimes, I'm completely wrong. The point is that your first outline is rarely more than a good starting point to help you get your thoughts in order.

One thing your outline will reveal is where you'll need more information. You might find yourself winding into a really great discussion area, but in doing so, discover that this is an area where you might need to return to the rabbit hole. Some authors will say that this means you've found a dead end, and you need to go back to the start of the maze. I say this a great opportunity to reveal your discovery to the readers with the same awe it's giving you at this moment. The fact that you are learning something about which you are passionate may indicate that other individuals have never considered this particular view or aspect of the same topic. You can avoid the unknown, or write it into your discussion because it is unknown.

Once you've got an outline that you're satisfied with or at least one that doesn't give you massive anxiety, you'll be able to see more clearly what thoughts you have about your topic. From here, you can decide what angle you'll take to discuss your topic.

Another common misconception regarding works of nonfiction is that they do not contain any opinions or bias. This is not true across the board. A travel journal, for example, has no choice but to be written from the point of view of the person traveling. It's impossible to be unbiased when you're writing about your own experiences from your own perspective.

In other cases, however, it's a good idea to remain as unprejudiced as possible with a catalogue-like approach, but that's entirely dependent upon the angle you wish to take.

The "angle" is how you will go about investigating your topic. For example, in this book, I've chosen to go with a very candid, casual approach to the topic of "how to write a book." I chose this angle because I think there are enough formal books on the topic, and I imagine there are quite a few people who need a friendly voice who knows what they're talking about to push them into doing the deed once and for all.

When it comes to your book, will you approach it as a passionate argument? A desperate plea? A scientific study? A historical collage? A gentle coaxing? One example I like to use when explaining different angles is that of the self-help book. Some of us need to be yelled at in order to get our lives straight. Others need to be subconsciously guided by subtext that allows us to make our own decisions. What style are you going to use to approach your topic?

The angle will also become evident from the outline you have created. You may have originally thought that you were going to do a completely unbiased history of birth control methods, only to realize somewhere in the creation of the outline that you simply cannot avoid including your own emotions and opinions on the topic. That doesn't mean you've chosen a bum topic; it simply means you will need to adjust your angle.

One way to approach your angle is to ask yourself "what do I want my audience to take away from this book?" In the example mentioned earlier, "a biographical account exploring Billy the Kid's role in establishing the economy of the Wild West," do you want them to have a higher opinion of Billy the Kid or a less favorable impression of early American economical values? You have the ability to guide the audience to understanding the topic in a certain light. You can't necessarily make them agree with you or change their own appreciation of the topic, but you do want them to feel they understand your own insight regarding the topic. The angle you choose takes the reader on a very specific voyage, so make sure they know exactly what to pack to take the trip alongside you.

At this point, you've chosen your topic. You've constructed your outline. You've examined your outline to get a feel for your angle. Now it's time to revisit everything you've done so far and get it fully organized to create the map of where you're heading.

From your outline, you should be able to create a working table of contents for your book. Your table of contents may not follow the same flow as your final outline, because your angle may have changed the manner in which your discussion occurs. Additionally, you may look at your outline and discover it doesn't actually fit the schematics of basic chapters after all.

Much as your first outline isn't necessarily your final outline, your first table of contents doesn't have to be your last either. I simply suggest that you turn your outline into a rudimentary draft of your table of contents to help you discover the order in which you'll be writing your book. In nonfiction, point tends to lead to point, and facts support arguments, which means you might find yourself backtracking if you were to write things in a specific order. Make sure your discussion or argument is presented in an order that makes sense based on your angle. Take your Uncle Lester, for example. The topic of the story is how he became "The Amazing Parcheezi." Perhaps you take the angle that he was absolutely destined to earn this moniker based on events that happened throughout his life. In this regard, presenting your details chronologically starting with his birth and continuing through how he lived up to the nickname following its bestowal would make sense.

Of course, there are many topics that don't lend themselves to any type of chronology. That's why taking the time to reorganize yourself will help you create a cohesive journey through your topic and lend further merit to your angle. I've included a few techniques to help guide you through some possibilities for your own nonfiction work in the "Resources" section, but for now, consider the overall "case" you're presenting. What is your thesis, or the point you're trying to prove (if any)? That should be stated in your introduction, or at the very beginning of the book. Then, think of the facts that lead towards that particular conclusion. Which is the strongest? Which is going to take the greatest amount of time to discuss? Can you create an equally long chapter for each fact, or are some of them technically sub-facts that could nestle closely with a larger, more pressing piece of information?

Putting together a nonfiction book is somewhat like putting together a jigsaw puzzle; however, while a puzzle has a definite singular correct solution, your book does not. The final format that you settle upon is beneficial to you, as it will make the flow of your writing feel much more familiar and be gentle on your brain as you compile your massive piles of facts. At the same time, the organization of your book should make sense for your reader as well. Your reader doesn't want to be confused, overwhelmed, underwhelmed, or feel like they're losing their mind. For example, if you're bringing up a particular example several times throughout a book, either consider a different arrangement or acknowledge this for your reader. I recall a particular example from earlier in my career, wherein certain aspects of a specific city were mentioned six times throughout the book. On the second mention, I thought perhaps I needed a nap. On the third use, I thought I might be going a little mad. By the fourth time this information popped up, I actively started flipping through the book to make sure I wasn't losing my mind. Sometimes this is unavoidable, but make sure you alert the reader. And try not to use the exact same sentences over again. Readers hate that.

You may be thinking that this is a lot of favors for your reader, and that's somewhat true. But what is the purpose of a book if not for the reader? We've discussed the concept of an "audience" a few times so far, so you have considered for whom you're writing the book and what purpose you want it to serve. But now I'm telling you that you have to reorganize your entire outline just so the readers will like it?

If you never intend anyone to read your book, then really, you don't need to follow any of this advice-- just go for it! Stop reading this at once and go make your dreams come true!

For the rest of us, however, who at least want their book to go over well at the family holiday party, creating a flow of details throughout your piece is crucial to gaining the appreciation of the reader. Have you ever started reading a book, only to stop halfway through because it wasn't capturing your attention? That experience is exactly why you need to at least somewhat include the reader in the experience of writing a book.

Ultimately, the act of writing is a bit of compromise between the author and the reader. You're going to write the book you want to write with the understanding that the resulting product should be something the reader wants to read. Believe it or not, that's usually easier than you might imagine.

Research, Resources, and Interviews

It almost goes without saying that a work of nonfiction will require substantial research. There are always facts to validate, points to prove, and references to include in your work to support your writing.

Even in the case of a personal work, such as a memoir or travelogue, you'll help substantiate your information with factual details. For example, rather than vaguely mentioning that Uncle Lester was born in a summer month at the turn of the century, you'll gain more credibility by saying he celebrates each July 29th. In the travelogue example, you'll greatly aid your reader and yourself by being able to mention where you are, where you're going, and how you're getting there.

There are unknown details about everything, even if you consider yourself a walking encyclopedia on a particular topic. At the end of this book, you'll find a "Resources" section. I would love to say that those are links that I exclusively hand-picked for my dear readers so they can grow and blossom as writers, but for the most part, they're the materials I used myself to organize my thoughts and make sure I wasn't telling you a bunch of bologna. I truly want you to grow and blossom, which is why I made it a point to share with you only information that I myself would use.

Since this is rarely a situation where "any old resource will do," it's a fantastic idea to really take your time in the research stage. I personally recommend looking up even the facts that you feel you know for certain, for the mere fact of corroborating your data with multiple resources. For example, I recently wrote a piece about a subject I know so well, I've been certified in it several times. In theory, I could have simply sat down and written a stream of consciousness brain dump of everything I know, and it would have been true. But it wouldn't have been good, and I wouldn't have had the facts on board.

Another great thing research can do is remind you of other things that go hand-in-hand with your main points. Sometimes, as writers, our focus is so strictly placed upon a particular piece of information that we block out knowledge that goes hand-in-hand with those facts. It's very much a "forest-and-trees" situation, wherein you're drilling down to a certain point so enthusiastically that you forget to mention all of the supporting details that are really important to the cause. Once upon a time, I was called upon to host a dinner for some prospective clients. They were chefs, so I wanted to serve some simple but flavorful foods to demonstrate that I had been paying attention and done my research on the topic they were pitching to me that evening. I found some very reputable resources, and I followed the recipes to the absolute letter. Nearly everything turned out beautifully, except for one particular dish. It looked nothing like the photos. Instead of looking like a fluffy beige spread, it was a wet, lumpy brown mess.

When my guests arrived, I had no choice but to serve it. I explained the situation and tried to laugh it off. They asked if I had done this and that while making it. I had not. "This" and "that" were not mentioned anywhere in the recipe I had followed. We took a look at my resource together and discovered that in the author's zest for explaining the history and cultural importance of the dish, they forgot to mention that the reader was supposed to peel a certain ingredient at a very specific time in the process.

The moral of this story is twofold:

1. Do not lose focus of a really important fact
2. Double-check your resources

It is far too easy to stop researching when you find the information you want. If something seems a bit untoward, it usually is. If I had looked for another recipe, I would have very quickly discovered the missing data. Instead, I looked at what I had and said, "Good enough!" While my prospective clients found the whole thing hilarious and hired me anyway, consider how your book will be received by people who don't know you directly and aren't able to hear your apologies and justifications for the error. Write it right the first time and earn reader trust for a lifetime.

On the topic of author accountability, resources can always be a bit of a mixed bag. In addition to spreading vast information, we're more aware than ever that the internet can also make misinformation viral in mere moments. This is another reason I like to recommend fact-checking nearly everything. From updates within the scientific community that invalidate previous theories, to updates in details surrounding your topic, it's never a bad idea to see what the community at large believes to be the "truth." Some inaccuracies may be unavoidable-- imagine writing an article about the Golden State Killer being at large on April 23, 2018, just one day before police announced they had arrested

Joseph DeAngelo for the crimes. I had the pleasure of writing a long piece about a particular celebrity's emotional quest for motherhood that was published the very same day she announced her pregnancy. The saving grace for my career and that of the publisher of that particular outlet was that the rest of my article was a well-researched compilation of her own words on the matter. I was accused of knowing the future, but that's entirely not true!

Another type of resource that can be both a blessing and a curse is an interview. If you can get a first-hand account of anything related to your topic, it will lend credibility and integrity to your piece. Except for one small problem: Interviewees aren't always accurate. That's not to say that they're all filthy liars, but just that we are all human. We remember things incorrectly. Details can get blurry over time and multiple retellings. We may start to confuse situations and transpose a few ingredients within our memories. And yes, some people are filthy liars.

Additionally, there's the interesting phenomenon in which experts might not agree. I encourage anyone who is conducting interviews to get as much perspective as possible on the topic you'll be discussing before actually starting the interview. If they can't get five out of five members of the American Dental Association to agree on the efficacy of a toothbrush, there's not the tiniest chance you'll find two identical versions of the same event.

If you choose to incorporate interviews in your research process, it's a great idea to get contact information so you can follow up with your subject. You may feel you've had an incredibly thorough discussion, yet as you write, you'll realize you didn't really catch the tone of a particular answer, or the subtext of a response isn't completely clear. If you have the opportunity to clarify that quote or notion, you'll avoid misrepresenting the truth.

So, how do you conduct an interview? First, research. Understand what you're going to be talking to this expert about. The most comfortable, informational, and overall successful interviews are more like conversations than a question and answer session. You don't have to reach a level of expertise on the topic, but at least know enough that you can participate in a discussion and ask clarifying questions that make sense. There's the famous example of the interviewer who was unaware that Paul McCartney had been in a band before Wings. Just a little bit of research can avoid awkward scenarios such as those.

Next, make sure you're interviewing your subject in a manner that is comfortable for both of you. I learned early in my career that I am incredibly awkward on the telephone. I'd rather take a red-eye flight to Buxtehude for an in-person interview than participate in a lengthy telephone interview. However, if I send my subject some questions via email, I'm more than happy to have a follow-up discussion via telephone. It's strange, I know.

The process of talking to an expert can be somewhat terrifying. Think of it as a conversation. Prepare a list of questions to get you started, but also jot down a list of points you would like to cover throughout the interview. Don't ignore the humanity of your subject. Phrases like, "You must have been surprised when you discovered…," or "What was going through your mind when…," or "What was it like to experience…," can give you loads of insight into the interviewee's relationship with the subject at hand and put a very relatable spin on even the most far-out topics. I once had to interview an investigator who had solved a serial murder and arrested the killer. I asked exactly one question. The rest of the time, we talked about his role in the crime itself, his headspace since the trial, and his relationship with fellow investigators. At the end of our hour-long chat, he asked if he could contact me again in the future when he was ready to write his autobiography. A good interview can be an amazing experience for everyone involved.

When you're using interviews in your nonfiction work, remember that nonfiction is supposed to reflect reality. The absence of fiction is truth. There are plenty of situations in which parts of interviews are specifically edited, decontextualized, and misconstrued in order to fit the author's angle. I certainly understand why some writers would choose to do this. To an extent, we all wiggle the truth a bit to get the desired results in life and writing. However, depending on the platform you're using to distribute this not-entirely-true information, there may be consequences. While defamation-- specifically libel-- is treated differently around the world, at the bare minimum it will be a dark mark on your writing career.

Writers have argued since the dawn of the written word whether fiction or nonfiction is "harder" than the other. Having written both myself, I have my own feelings on this matter, but for now, this is going to be one of those debates that may never end. Every author has a comfort zone, which means certain pieces will be much "easier" to write than others. "Easier" can mean many things to different people: faster to write, less stressful, minimal research, or bountiful source material. Sadly, it remains true that some books are pleasure cruises while others are as enjoyable as the tour of the S.S. Minnow. That's not to say that all books are a boat wreck, but that some books are a struggle from the first word and may turn out very different than intended.

Therefore, reflect back to that "sense of humor" I mentioned as a requirement for writing a book. While I've equipped you with various strategies and tools to help guide you through the pre-work of both fiction and nonfiction pieces, please don't believe that any of these are a "one and done" scenario. Don't fool yourself into thinking you can slot "pre-work for my novel" on your calendar as a brief afternoon chore. This will take time and energy, as also mentioned earlier. The sense of humor is the manna that will sustain your spirit while you wrestle with the reality of how onerous the pre-work process can be.

How you conduct your pre-work is entirely up to you. Many authors get the entire text laid out-- at least a preliminary version-- before they start writing. Others may find that they've organized them into a good space to write a particular section right this second, which they can edit back in once they've got a final structure in place. Use the method that works best for you. This isn't strictly a knitting project or a quilting project; instead, "Writing is the art of letting the muse soar brightly," as a former mentor of mine put it. For your first piece, you may wish to tinker around with your order of operations and structure as you discover what works best for you and your train of thought.

Each book you write will involve a certain amount of experimentation. While doing the pre-work will help you prepare for writing a book, don't feel that everything you've done is carved into stone. As mentioned earlier, it is possible that you will change some very important details in your book as it develops on the page whether you're writing a fiction piece or a work of nonfiction. When things change, don't feel that you've failed in your pre-work or that these outlines and hours of research were all in vain. If anything, learning what you don't want to do with your book makes it that much more satisfying when you discover the direction you prefer to take instead.

Whether you end up following these steps exactly or using them as the basis for your own unique process, keep in mind that the goal here is to provide you with direction for your new project. Many first time authors become frustrated early in the writing process, simply because they haven't done sufficient work ahead of time. The great news is that you can always stop what you're doing mid-sentence, leave yourself a bookmark or note to return to, and revisit your notes. Maybe your character map wasn't quite as accurate as you had envisioned. Maybe your angle is slightly askew. Revisit. Regroup. Relax.

You may feel like the pre-work is never-ending, especially if you find yourself revisiting and regrouping more than once. That's not a bad thing at all. It's simply preparing you for the next step of the process which is setting sail on this monumental voyage. The next step, of course, is to sit down and write a book.

Surviving The Writing Process

To write a book, begin in a comfortable seated position. Make sure you have a laptop, computer, device, pen and paper, quill and scroll, or whatever media in which you wish to write. Close your eyes. Take a deep breath. Exhale slowly. Open your eyes. Write a book. The end.

If only it were that simple! In truth, there will be days when writing comes as naturally to you as breathing or swallowing. Other days, you'll feel nauseated just knowing that the written word exists. There have been times when I've been irked by the label on a packet of snacks simply because it had the audacity to include words and sentences.

The term "surviving" may seem a little dramatic or hyperbolic, but I find that writing is an activity of survival for the author and the piece equally. If you give up on writing your book, then the story does not live on. Equally, if you become so frustrated with the process that you swear off writing anything more significant than your name on a birthday card, your development of a passion and talent has terminated. While writing a book is unlikely to be fatal, the knocks you feel during the process might bring an end to the whole endeavor entirely. If you quit, it shouldn't be because continuing would ruin your life but because you've tried writing, and it's simply not for you.

As always, you'll need time, energy, and a sense of humor which will apply to the various skills that will help you retain your passion for this project even as the days drag on and words start to lose their meaning. In the following chapters, we'll look at some of the things that help writers retain the desire to write, even if the words aren't coming. They may seem a bit obvious at first, but when you're facing a blank white page, the urge to panic is very strong, especially during your inaugural attempt.

In this section, we'll explore some of the best ways to not panic, stay focused, and keep your eyes on the prize of successfully completing that very first book.

Chapter 1: Staying Organized

While it's true that the concept of organization has been mentioned more than a few times already, it really can't be mentioned enough when outlining the process of writing your first book.

The temptation to just open a journal or online word processing document and start writing will be strong. In fact, I highly recommend you follow this urge from time to time, especially when creativity or passion starts waning. The only downfall to this method is that when writing with our eyes closed, we tend to lose sight of where we were trying to go in the first place. This is a great way to get the words flowing, but you might also produce a whole bunch of drivel.

One technique for helping yourself stay accountable when going on these writing sprints involves a little extra organization. Each time you sit down to write, I encourage you to take a few moments to read what you wrote in your previous session. Take a look at your notes, reference your character map and plot outline for fiction pieces, or glance back to the final draft of your table of contents for nonfiction writers.

A book, with its thousands of words and hundreds of pages, is overwhelming. It's a long journey full of twists and turns and points and counterpoints. So, try to think of it as an adventure with a destination that's still far in the distance. Imagine you're going to drive a car from Seattle, Washington to Boca Raton, Florida. That's a trip of approximately 3,200 miles, which is approximately 48 hours of continuous driving. Looking at it like that, it seems incredibly overwhelming to take on a trip like that, and you might immediately start looking for the fastest and least expensive flight.

But instead of looking at it as two days of endless driving, remember your humanity. You'll need to stop every so often to eat, fuel up the car, and use the restroom. It's in your best interest to pause once in a while to get a bit of rest, lest your eyes glaze over and your brain go on auto-pilot. Therefore, it is far more likely that you'll break up the voyage into small, manageable pieces. You'll drive for a few hours the first day, see how the car is handling. Stop for fuel when you need it, pop into the station for a drink or snack. Pause at rest areas to use the facilities, walk around a little bit, maybe take a little nap.

Once you relax and let yourself absorb the beauty of the journey itself, you'll start enjoying it more. Maybe you'll stop at a restaurant that you've always wanted to try. You might choose to wander through a town a bit while you're there, dashing into the shops for a little local flavor. Of course, there might be days when it rains, or you're just not feeling the spirit of adventure, when you just want to put the pedal to the metal and get on with it, but that's part of the journey too.

As someone who has made several cross-continental voyages and written just as many books (including a book that I wrote while driving the entirety of the American East Coast), I'm always struck by how similar both processes are. The only major difference is that you can write a book in a stationary position, without leaving the house.

When you open your journal or device and gaze upon that blank page, don't think about how monumental this task is. Don't think about how long it will take you to reach your goal, or how inconvenient it's going to be to make the trip. Instead, break it down into small pieces, just like you would your road trip.

Your first day writing, focus on the introduction. Don't overthink it-- just start driving. Tune out the part of your brain that's screaming, "This is madness! This is too big! This is going to take too long! You're out of your element!" Lock your mental GPS on the first point you want to make in your book, and go for it.

Your introduction is going to set the tone for your book, and if you've created loads of notes during your pre-work, it will be the most honest and forthright thing you write. You haven't had the time to come up with preconceived notions about what you're writing. You haven't developed your voice entirely, you're just pecking along, trying to explain what you're about to write to a reader who has no idea you're even writing a book. The whole process is a mystery at this point. Good thing you have plenty of notes.

Just as you certainly wouldn't attempt to drive from Seattle to Boca Raton without GPS, an atlas, a compass, or some type of tool to help you find the way, the notes you assembled during your pre-work are going to act as a map to guide you through your book. Use this map to help you find your way point-by-point, just as you would make your way across the United States stop-by-stop. Perhaps today you write through Chapter 1, or the point in the plot where the main character is introduced. The next time you sit down, you'll get through Chapter 2, or take the main character to the point where the main conflict is revealed.

Set some very specific points, and write each day until you've completed that portion of your journey. What will make this strategy work, of course, is your ongoing commitment to organization. When you use a GPS or map to plan a road trip, you plot out your points. You check the roads and get a feel for the highways and byways you need to take in order to get to your next checkpoint. You don't look all the way to your final destination; you take your time finding your way. You stay with your map at all times. Sure, you might end up following a detour, or discover a more scenic route, but you have a specific place towards which you are heading.

Your pre-work, research, and any notes you make along the way are your map. They tell you where you should go next. Let them do their job. Don't leave your notes in a drawer, or decide you were out of your mind and throw them away, or tell yourself you can fly without a map. Once you get into a good flow, you might not need your notes every moment, but given that each session of writing is nearly always different from the day before, there will come a time when you'll deeply crave those notes again.

One particular trick that has saved me a lot of time and tears is to keep a writing journal. You might be thinking, "I'm already writing, and you want me to write some more? You're out of your mind." It does sound like overkill, I'll admit. But the purpose of a writing journal can actually be very simple-- to make notes of what you do each day when writing.

By "journal," I don't necessarily mean a bound notebook type of thing, though that system does tend to work for many writers, especially those early in their career. You can use a system of comments and highlight text in a word processing program, or actual sticky notes if you're handwriting your manuscript. Whatever it takes for you to recognize, record, and revisit points in the process where you had to pause to think about things is as fine a method as any, because you're not keeping a writing journal for anyone but yourself.

Writing is not necessarily a chronological thing, even if the piece you are writing is very strictly chronologically structured. You might be knee deep in Chapter 12, only to realize that life is going to be a lot easier for your characters if you go back and change something slightly in Chapter 3. On the nonfiction front, you might discover that an argument you made in a previous section was weak where it was sitting, and you clearly need to relocate it to a later section, where it actually enhances the discussion. When you make changes like these, make note of them in your writing journal. Examples of these notes might include things like:

> "1, February: Changed April's hair color to brown, starting in Chapter 5. Had her dye it so Rebel doesn't recognize her in Chapter 8."

Or in nonfiction:

> "25, October: Moved 'Billy the Kid's horse, etc...' from Section 3: Livestock to Section 7: Tradeable Wares. Livestock section now focuses on cattle and farm life. Chickens going under trade as well, though mentioning them in "Marketable Goods" section of Livestock section."

The goal of these notes, and the journal as a whole, is that it will help you not only recognize changes you made in your draft, but will also help you remember *why* you did that in the first place. Sure, you can set up your word processing software to track all changes, but it can't capture your internal argument as you try to make a decision.

The concept of organization extends beyond the notes and to the mental notes and dialogue you're having with yourself as you write your book. There will come times when you type out an entire page, then freeze and think, "Is that even what I wanted to say?" Being organized in both your notes and your thought process will help you sort out what you're doing. And being able to remain in synchrony with yourself through the days, months, and years it may take you to write a book is the only way I can think of to continue your productivity through thick and thin.

Chapter 2: Being Productive

The original title of this chapter was "Staying on Deadline." In my mind, I was going to explain to you how to budget time to get your first draft done within a specific timeframe. But, as I've preached to you frequently throughout this text, changes do happen.

Instead of teaching you how to force yourself to write when your brain says "no" but the calendar says "yes," I'd rather encourage you to develop a passion for productivity. Truly talented writers can spirit up an entire text from nothing in a matter of seconds, but that's not the experience you should have for your first book. Rather, your first book should be an effort you undertake because you truly want to. It should be positive and passionate, and whether or not you choose to ever write another book, you should walk away from the process proud of yourself for having done something so monumental.

As I mentioned earlier, you should set a timeline for yourself simply to keep your brain aware of the fact that this is a real thing, and it does deserve your attention. How strict you are with your deadline depends on how well you know yourself. Some of us need pressure to thrive, which means being a little aggressive with deadlines in order to keep yourself focused and excited about your writing. On the other hand, you might avoid excess anxiety by allowing yourself generous milestones that simply demonstrate you are making forward motion, rather than wallowing in each potential sticky spot.

Regardless of your expectations, the main goal of setting a timeline is to promote writing. When writing their first book, nearly every writer I've spoken to says the same thing: We start obsessing about whether it's good, interrupt ourselves, rewrite the same paragraph eight times, give up because it's too hard, wonder if we're failures at everything we try, spiral into self-doubt, and basically have a very bad time. Instead of making it good on the first pass, just concentrate on making it.

You want to write a good book, but before it can be good, it must be a book. Write it. Just write the blessed thing! Just like you'd step on the gas and speed away from a roach-infested hotel room on a cross-country roadtrip, sometimes it's best to keep moving forward and not look back when writing.

Make adjustments. Pay attention to detours. Take the scenic route. But don't spend too much time glancing back at where you've been until you really know where you're going. If you're going along at a nice clip in the introductory pages and suddenly remember that April's hair is going to change color, don't stop. Use that writing journal to make note of it and keep going. There might be a reason why your brain wanted you to write it this way now. Explore that, but make note of it, in case you don't like where that path leads. You wouldn't turn off your GPS when you get lost, and you wouldn't stop where you are, turn off the car, and call it quits, either. You can always come back when you have more time and fuel.

Remember as you write that when you come back later, you'll have a fuller grasp of what (if anything) needs to be changed. You could go back on April's hair throughout the entire book. What if you discover, just as you're wrapping things up, that April really enjoys changing her hair color, and she does it a few times throughout the tale in order to be more of a social chameleon? You've just realized that you need to revisit every mention of April's hair color to make sure it fits the social situation in that scene. Things like this happen, so make notes, come back later, and go forward for now.

You'll also need to examine your relationship with the word "progress." Earlier, we discussed how the recommended 2,000 words each day might not make sense for you, at least not on a daily basis. I encourage you to gauge progress not by how many words you write each day, but by the things you actually accomplish when you do sit down to write. If you only write 100 words, but you manage to get yourself through a section that was particularly troublesome for you, that's progress! If you do a 4,000 word sprint because you haven't had the time to sit down and write for yourself in weeks, that's also progress!

Many people get a little frenzied during their first attempt to write something substantial. If discipline helps you thrive, then by all means, create a stringent program for yourself. I find that if my deadlines are too far in the future, I will almost dare myself to wait until the last minute. But, if I choose instead to force myself to make some form of progress each day, I procrastinate less, and I love my final product more. That being said, giving myself a very specific quantity of words to accomplish each time I sit down would only exacerbate my anxiety. I'm more of the "write until your head is empty" type of writer when I have my druthers. Writing, in a professional capacity, has helped me learn how to hold myself more accountable to a schedule, but hopefully your first book won't come with a tight deadline!

In preparing for your first book, though, you may not really know what your style is like. You may have never sat down and written thousands of words at once, or if you have, it may have been long, long ago. It's not the type of thing everyone gets to enjoy in their personal or professional life, so it may feel very strange at first.

In fact, it might quite literally feel strange, as in physically uncomfortable. If you're not familiar with typing, your fingers and wrists might become sore or achy after a particularly long stretch of typing. Handwriting your book can also lead to aches and pains in the wrists and fingers. If you don't usually sit for hours on end, your spine and posterior may start to object to your new pastime.

Keep in mind that writing is actual exercise for your mind as well as your body. Just as you wouldn't enter a marathon if you've never jogged down your driveway, you'll need to give yourself time to adjust to this new activity, both mentally and physically. You might find yourself feeling exhausted at the end of a writing session or wired from a burst of endorphins as you try a new task. No one told me about how writing can affect the body, so I was completely surprised when I burst out crying inconsolably for half an hour after submitting my final draft. Your brain will be taxed. You might forget things. You might find yourself on edge. You might find it difficult to sleep or to rise. These are all very real side effects of writing your first book.

Over time, the process will become easier, but you need to train yourself to endure it. Take breaks to avoid actual writer's cramps. I like to get up and walk around the room every thirty minutes or so. I wait until I've reached a good stopping point, of course, but then I close my eyes, do some desk stretches, and get up for a good minute or two. Sitting on an exercise ball instead of a regular chair is a great way to avoid the pitfalls of poor posture when seated. In the "Resources" section, I've included a few links to exercises you can do to keep your body as limber as your mind during the writing process.

Sometimes, if I find my mind blank, I'll turn to the internet and read something related to my topic, just to get the brain juices going. When I was writing heavily for the automotive community, I would pause work to watch episodes of *Top Gear* or *Rust Valley Restorers* to refresh my appreciation of writing in the right tone and voice. Don't beat your poor brain into submission over this task; instead, let it be a part of the instrument and play for the muses naturally. Alternately, I'll shut off the computer and do some Yoga Nidra to prevent my brain from going into overdrive. Find what helps you think-- I've included a few suggestions for brain cleansing activities in the "Resources" section. It's important to cleanse the mind from time to time to keep your mental focus and emotions in check.

Give yourself time to focus on learning your own process. By emphasizing the overall accomplishment of any progress at all, you're giving yourself the room you need to learn your own needs.

Your procedures will start to fall into place as you become more familiar with your mental, emotional, and physical needs. Make adjustments. I can't tell you how many playlists I auditioned before I found the exact tunes I needed to be productive.

Seasoned authors across the board recommend finding a good place in which you can do your writing. A quiet spot, where no one can bother you and you don't find yourself tempted by too many distractions can be incredibly helpful in inspiring and maintaining productivity. This doesn't mean you need to build yourself a state-of-the-art office, unless you truly want to. Many a bestseller has been written at a kitchen table, behind a blanket "wall" in the living room, on a closet floor, or in the dark once the kids have gone to sleep. Part of finding your groove is finding a good place to work. If you find yourself being very easily distracted, move. Set yourself up for success; trying to "push through" a situation that just isn't working will only bring distaste for the overall experience.

Over time, your progress will become a process, and your process will in turn raise your productivity. The muscles that ached and the tears that were shed will all become more rare, as your body learns to sit and the mind becomes accustomed to this exciting task. You'll feel less forced, frantic, and formal and more focused. You'll look forward to your writing time. Knowing that you'll return to a sort of normalcy or even a state of bliss after that first major roadbump of entering unfamiliar territory should help you keep your eyes on the prize, so to speak. Travel one stop at a time, but if you remind yourself that you're moving forward, the journey will be all the more enjoyable and rewarding once you've reached its end.

Chapter 3: Dealing with Changes

By now, you might be a little confused about the methods I'm prescribing for you: Always go forward, except when you turn around and go back, but always make notes about why you did, then go forward again. In fact, that's a pretty accurate description of the writing process, but since this is your first time, I'll try to simplify it a bit.

Always go forward. Progress is good. Write more words, make more of your book appear before you, continue momentum, and so forth. The more you write, the greater the chance that you'll work yourself through those moments of confusion and self-doubt. Always end the session with more words than when you started.

However, change is inevitable. We must not fear change. You will wake up one morning and realize that you didn't include a certain detail earlier, and you need to add it. Do just that. Note it in your journal, and then continue forward. Don't spend an excessive amount of time re-reading what you've already done, because you've got an entire revision and editing process for that. When you go back to make essential changes, I strongly encourage you to put blinders on to the rest of what you've written, at least for that moment. Make your change, make sure it exists peacefully with the surrounding text, and then return to the prospect of forward motion.

But the concept of "change" isn't strictly limited to parts already written. As you move ever boldly forward, get ready for things to get weird. Your characters may turn out to be totally different from your first impressions. You may find that something you considered irrefutable truth was proven incorrect recently. In this great journey of writing, there will be roadblocks and detours you never intended to take.

So, how do you deal with unexpected change, especially when you're supposed to be the one in control here? This is one of the very few scenarios in which I would encourage you, as a writer, to pause briefly. The other scenarios include natural disasters, fire, and medical emergencies, but this is one of the few instances when you have a free pass to stop yourself before you proceed past the point of no return. If you have discovered a major gap in reality, you have permission to stop and regroup.

By "major gap in reality," I am referencing situations in fictional pieces including but not limited to:

- Your character's personality has changed so drastically, they cannot realistically perform the plot as drafted
- The survival of a character is dependent on your decisions, and you hadn't initially planned to write a mortal departure
- You're reaching the ending far sooner than you expected
- The original ending you planned is completely unlikely
- The genre skipped track on you, and in order to follow the new version, you need to do more research

For nonfiction writers, you might encounter the following, and then some:
- Your main argument is based on a fact that has been proven false
- In writing a particular section, you discovered you have a very unequal distribution of information compared to the rest of the sections
- You're making the same point and argument repeatedly, but not in an informative manner
- You're bleeding a rock with your resources
- Your interviewees stop responding to you, and now you have absolutely no idea how their story ends

As you can see, these are not mere "situations" but occurrences that would require major edits to everything that you have written and will continue to write. Think of it as a subconscious railroad switch, gently guiding your barreling train to another track without missing a beat. You may have thought you were the engineer of this particular train, but surprise! Something happened along the way, and you're in an entirely different place.

This does not necessarily mean you should jump ship and abandon your work. In each case, you can revise the text to suit the new situation, if you feel it is for the better. That means you'll have to revisit your initial plans as well as the developing text in order to find all of the bits that are impacted by this update. Sometimes, you'll find that you can actually tie it all together simply by moving forward. For example, in a situation where my interviewees ghosted me, I was able to take the information they had given me in our first sessions, flip the hypothesis of the article, adjust my gaze a bit, and create an even more interesting article because of my changes. Don't give up. Don't be shocked. Look at your piece and think, "What can I make that's even better?"

But sometimes, you're completely blindsided by the change. You can't understand why a particular character comes across as cruel and narcissistic because you've always intended her to be the self-sacrificing character. Your heroine is annoying, and it seems like the characters are less and less interested in the rising action each day. In the nonfiction world, you might discover you're practically shouting your text, trying to impress upon your reader how important this detail is, or you're repeating phrases verbatim unintentionally. You might look at your book in utter fear, wondering how on Earth did this happen? Who wrote this?

First, know that this is very natural. It can be a bit unsettling when you look at something you've produced, and it is very much not like you expected it at all. Sometimes what our mind's eye sees is completely exempt from replication in the real world, especially when we add our own perspective to it. It sounds a little scary or supernatural, but the way you feel in your own world can very easily be reflected in what you write. Have you ever cleaned the house angrily, or washed the dishes when you were really happy? The way we feel has a lot to do with how we act, and when the duty at hand is translating your own imagination into the written word… Well, a funny thing happened on the way to the paper.

The more you write, the easier it will be to avoid this phenomenon because you'll recognize how you write when you're mad, sad, lonely, anxious, or slightly tipsy on white wine. There will be subtle changes in your style, and the developments in your text will start to reflect the way you're reacting in real life. We write what we know, and if you're having a bad day, you'll use your characters as a sounding board, or your arguments might become a little more impassioned.

This is another reason why I recommend you keep moving forward as much as possible. The energy you bring to the pages when you write is important for productivity, and it can become very stagnant as you continue forward. If you're dealing with something in your private life, keep writing, even if your original concepts change. Likewise, there will be chapters that bore you. Push forward through this to see what comes out on the other side. Your energy is what will keep a book churning forward. When you stop this energy to linger too long on something that's already been done, you lose forward momentum. Your energy changes. The moment is lost. See where things go, and if it turns out that the inadvertent turn at the station wasn't for the best, first decide where you can go along this route.

When it comes to writing your first book, something will inevitably change. It may be the contents of the book, or it may be your own perspective. Don't fear change, follow it. And when it becomes clear that you need to reassess, do so. What you build upon your current structure is only going to better it. But for the love of everything, make notes about it so you don't lose your train of thought or the steam to continue.

Perhaps this was not the outline of "the writing process" you wanted. You might have been looking for someone to help you put one word after the other. Maybe you wanted to know what the best adjectives are, or how to really use adverbs to spice up your writing. Those are very important things to know as a writer, after all!

While I don't disagree that writing is art with words, I also don't feel like I should be telling you how to execute your art. There is a lot about writing to me-- and to many others who write for a living-- that is still somewhat spiritual or sacred. I don't know why I love doing it. I don't know why it's always come so easily to me. I can't tell you where my brain goes, or where the words come from, or how I know exactly how I want to organize things. When a character is engaged in dialogue, I don't know who is really speaking to whom on a subconscious level. What I do know is that I can't imagine a way to force someone to let their brain flow into the written word. You just have to accept that it is your task and try it.

And that, more than anything, is my main piece of advice regarding writing: Try it. Don't look at what you've written and say, "Oh that's crap, and I'll never get better." The first time isn't meant to be good. The first few pages will be awkward. You'll be able to see the cracks where you might've stumbled and fudged it for a little bit because you weren't quite sure what was happening. Maybe you become hyperaware and self conscious and start doing the literary equivalent of stammering. That's okay! That happens all the time! In fact, that's exactly what the editing stage is for.

If you are expecting to produce Nobel prize-winning content the first time you even try to write, then I formally invite you to get over yourself. Write first, then perfect. Make the book, then make the book better. I'm not saying be lazy-- always give it your best effort and as much energy as you can muster-- but recognize that you are actually expected to go back and make changes.

In the next chapter, we'll learn how "edit" is much more than a "four letter word," despite the fact that it does contain four letters. Change is good. Edits are expected. You have an opportunity to clean the entire house before your company comes over, so take advantage of it.

The Editing Stage

According to the Merriam Webster's Dictionary:

"Definition of **Edit**

transitive verb

1a: to prepare (something, such as literary material) for publication or public presentation

edit a manuscript

b: to assemble (something, such as a moving picture or tape recording) by cutting and rearranging

edit a film

c: to alter, adapt, or refine especially to bring about conformity to a standard or to suit a particular purpose

carefully edited the speech

edit a data file"

As you read that, you may see that there is nothing in there linking editing to being a worthless writer. Because it's not true. Editing isn't necessary because you're a terrible person who deserves nothing good; editing is an opportunity to make sure what we've written is exactly right.

Somehow, a perceived notion has been grown that editing is bad, and only people who aren't very good at writing make edits. This, of course, is nonsense. If you care enough to swallow your pride, abandon your ego, and re-read everything you've written with the intention of making it even better, then you clearly care deeply about your book and want it to be the best it can be.

Also, for those for whom the reality hasn't quite set in yet: Congratulations; you've written a book.

When you reach the editing process, you have officially written a book. Now you get to make it a good book, and you shouldn't view that as punishment for not writing a book perfectly the first time through, but rather, as a privilege for following your passion and making this dream come true in the first place. If you can grind through the long and emotional process of writing the book, then certainly you can go through the thing again with a feather duster and a bit of polish!

Remember: Writing a book requires time, energy, and a sense of humor. It is in your best interest to extend these traits through the editing process as well. Let's take a look at some other things to keep in mind when entering and preceding through the editing phase of your book. And remember: It's just a phase!

Chapter 1: How to Ignore Your Instincts and Edit Subjectively

It is all too common to get that sinking-pit stomach feeling when you face the editing phase. You are going to come face to face with your own human fallibility, after all. It's one thing to emotionally prepare for the act of editing, but to actually do the chore is another thing altogether.

There are two typical reactions to facing the emotions that come with the first round of editing of your first book:

1. Tear it apart. Tear it all apart. Burn it and start over.
2. Put it in a box. Lock it. Throw away the key. Bury the box.

Neither of these are going to help you. Therefore, you need to learn how to ignore your instincts and simply edit your book.

There are different ways of going about it. If you've been keeping a writing journal, one of the first things you can do is read the journal, and then look back at all the parts you've referenced. Make sure April's hair is the correct color at all times. Be certain that Billy the Kid's horse isn't running amok throughout the text. If you changed a plot point or argument in the mid-to-later part of the book, make sure all earlier references have been updated as well. For those using a word processing program, the "Find" feature can come in very handy here.

Readers can forgive a lot of things and suspend their disbelief significantly, but inconsistencies are just annoying. Avoid annoying your reader. Do a read through of your book with the specific intention of making sure everything is consistent from chapter to chapter. And by "everything," I truly mean everything. Here are a few examples of things to check for when evaluating the consistency of your text:

- Is your tone and voice the same throughout the book, or did that energy from being in a different mood leak through, as I mentioned it might?
- Does the narrator or point of view of the text remain the same?
- Are all mentions of locations or settings accurate? (this is equally important for fiction and nonfiction works.)
- Are all names spelled the same way throughout the text, or annotations made where names may change purposefully? (Example: Referencing members of royalty is one situation in which individuals may have a given name, a familial nickname, one or more titular names, and so on. Let the readers know all of them, so it's not confusing when you switch between them.)
- Are all personal details, such as outward appearance, clothing/ style, personality, and other identifying characteristics unchanging OR do these details change appropriately at the right time and remain changed until otherwise specified?
- Does your treatment of various issues or scenarios align throughout the book?

- Is there anything you mention at some point in your introduction or thesis that immediately disappears?

Essentially, you want to read through your book and not once think, "Wait, what happened to ___?" Whether that blank is filled by an important historical reference, a character name, a recognizable tattoo, a dog, an interviewee, a significant resource, or a portion of your argument, don't let it dangle.

So how do you clean it up? Start with evaluation. Do you really need that thing that fills the blank to exist in the first place? What type of effort in the form of rewrites will be needed to re-establish consistency? While you may find that you can get rid of the offending disagreeable detail, it may be salvageable. You may, in fact, find that taking the time to do some pretty sizable rewrites to explain the inconsistency will not only eliminate confusion, but bolster your work altogether. Nearly every writer has had a cringe-worthy moment where they discovered a major boo-boo or blunder, only to write it into the text with great success.

Once you've got a thorough and complete text without any strange wandering threads that lead nowhere, it's time to address the language and grammar. If you're using a word processing program, you'll likely have minimal typos, unless you happen to make typos that actually make sense. I really need to send my editors a fruit basket at some point because they have caught me in the act of things that legitimately don't make sense because Google Docs autocorrected my typos to something similar but not right. You'll want to find those before you release your book to the outside world. Even if you never intend your text to see wide distribution, you do want to avoid hearing every person who does read the book say, "Did you know that on page 113, you used the word 'lighting' instead of 'lightning'?" And yes, that is a real example from my own career-- the error appeared in a commemorative handbook for a one-time event, and I thought I may never recover from my shock and disappointment at my mistake. But I did.

At this point, you have uncovered and corrected all glaring errors and omissions. If this is a low-stakes project, you may wish to press forward and pursue distribution of your project now, whether that means printing up booklets for your friends and family, or sending off a file to your loved ones. However, if you want to make a big splash with your first book, it's time to call in an outside party to read and evaluate your text. Sounds scary? It's absolutely terrifying, at least the first few times. But having a beta reader or editing team tear your book to bits is far less dehumanizing than reading negative reviews. Trust me.

Chapter 2: The Importance of Outside Readers

If you're concerned about letting other people read your work, imagine how I'm feeling right now. I'm writing a chapter about editing that will be edited by my long-suffering editors. Talk about working under pressure!

The truth of the matter is that I, personally, am thrilled when my work goes off to editors and beta readers. I feel like I write in a vacuum, typing out things that only I might ever want to read, so having a clean up crew to make what I write suitable for public consumption is a major relief to me. In fact, if a manuscript comes back without being shredded, redlined, and annotated, I become paranoid that I've done something wrong.

The purpose of an editor is to catch what you've missed. An ideal editor should have a strong background in language and grammar and understand the various current formats for both fiction and nonfiction pieces. I went to school in the 1980s. The styles we used back then are long gone, and the grammar guides that led to my high marks in literature and writing are now laughably out of date. I try to keep up, but then I throw out a super-casual, candid, conversational book like this one, and my poor editors suffer trying to make it fit a format. I would like to note that I am very, very sorry for their suffering, even though they'll likely remove one of those "verys" for being redundant.

Beta readers, on the other hand, are there to make sure your text works. They can provide editing and formatting corrections as necessary, but the primary goal of a beta reader is to make sure that the book works before anyone sees it. Much like a trusted friend evaluating your hair, makeup, and outfit before you leave the house for an important shindig, the beta reader ensures your slip isn't showing and there isn't lipstick on your teeth, metaphorically speaking.

The purpose of an editor or beta reader is to approach your book objectively, without any bias or preconceived notion. Therefore, you may not want a close friend, housemate, or partner to be your first reader, unless they are very good at separating the art from the artist. What I mean by that is someone who knows you very well will know your tone of voice, how you communicate, and even the subconscious nuances of the way you speak and think. They'll read your book in your voice, which will be beneficial for them, but not every reader will have that same understanding of your style.

If an editor or beta reader has done a very thorough job, they'll share their own insight into what they like about your book and what didn't work for them. I strongly encourage you to take this information into consideration. With a few exceptions, they aren't sharing their thoughts and recommendations to be mean, but rather because they have discovered opportunities for making your book even stronger.

Let your soul and your ego rest peacefully, knowing that this isn't an attack, but rather an invitation from a like-minded friend to make things even better than they are.

It is easy, as a writer, to write from your own point of view and understanding about a topic. Unfortunately, that makes assumptions about what the reader already knows and understands. Very rarely are these things universal. Therefore, when an editor or beta reader points out that the jump from point to point doesn't make sense, don't bother thinking, "No one understands me as a writer," but rather, "What can I do to make this clearer to my audience?" Remember that you're trying to create a clear picture of your intentions, regardless of whether you're writing fiction or nonfiction. Clarity is the best way to get your reader on board, so if those who are reading the book are having trouble following, it doesn't mean you're a horrible writer, but merely that you have some explaining to do.

I realize that can be a big jolt to the ego, especially when you've tried your best, and it's your first effort. But before you begin licking your wounds and avowing you'll never write again, pause for a moment and really read the comments you've received from your outside reader. It is very possible that they simply weren't the right reader for the assignment. It is also possible that they headed into it with a very different concept of what they were supposed to be doing. Any editor or beta reader worth their salt will leave a slew of comments and feedback about your work. You'll be able to tell from reading them not only what they objectively thought, but what they expected from your work as well. Sometimes-- however unintentional it may be-- what they want your book to be will differ from what's on the page, which will lead to a whole avalanche of misunderstanding and a lack of appreciation.

One way to mitigate this is to do a trial run with your outside reader. Send them a few pages. A chapter. See what they do with it. If they come back to you with feedback that makes sense, then you've got a good match, and you should run with it. Let them have at it and build a better book. Alternatively, if they clearly missed the point of the assignment, perhaps they should wait for the final product. They may be wonderful, perfectly intelligent people, but just as you wouldn't want to listen to an entire album in a musical style you loathe, forcing someone to read a book they just don't get is equally unfair, and no one will benefit from it. While you want your book to have the greatest appeal possible, truly nothing in this world is beloved by all.

My last piece of advice when it comes to working with editors,beta readers, and outside parties of all kinds is this: You don't always have to take their advice. At the end of the day, this is your book, filled with your ideas, research, time, energy, and sense of humor. At some point, you will need to decide for and by yourself that the book you have created is exactly the product you intended in the first place.

And that part is tough enough that it gets its own chapter.

Chapter 3: When to Call It "Done"

When I was a young person, studying writing in school, I hated what our professor called "rewind weeks." That week, instead of submitting a brand new piece for peer review and group discussion, we were to take a previous piece and make it new again. Hardly anyone liked it. One fellow, in particular, would do something delightfully subservient, like change a single character's appearance in a way that really didn't matter to the context of the story and leave everything else the same. One writer enjoyed rewriting his work so that the letter "e" wouldn't appear anywhere in the text. The rest of us, however, begrudgingly leafed through our portfolio to figure out what we could unenthusiastically turn into a new piece.

But here's the thing: We were all missing the point of the exercise. The whole reason why we were doing this was to drill home the lesson that any piece you write is going to be a reflection of who, where, what, and how you were at the time you wrote it. When you do massive revisions, it's usually because the version of yourself reading the book is markedly different from the person who wrote it in the first place. While you're welcome to do that, you need to know that you aren't required to do so.

Sometimes, it's best to just let a piece be. There have been many times when writers look at something and say, "That's crap. I'll have the editors deal with it." Again, apologies to my editors. But then the editors take a look at it and feel that it isn't crap at all. That's because we're our own worst critic, and we won't let things leave our grasp while we can still control everything about them. Sounds psychologically deep, but many of us are hardwired to be absolute control monsters, and that's ok.

Letting go of a manuscript is hard. I genuinely cried the first time I submitted a final draft, as I mentioned before. I was equal parts proud of myself, relieved that the process was done, and terrified that I had just unleashed a bunch of garbage on the literary community. The truth is that most of the things that are written will be sublimely enjoyed by many people, while others just don't care for it very much.

This does not mean you're a failure. Negative feedback and destructive criticism have nothing to do with you or your talents. If someone truly cares, they'll leave you constructive feedback and notes that can help you build upon them. Otherwise, they're just miserable people who want the world to know they've had an awful time.

Think of your favorite musical artist. Do you know how many people hate their work? Bach, Beethoven, The Beatles, Beck... for each of these artists there is someone out there who hates everything they've done with a passion so deep they could choke on it. But that doesn't mean they aren't talented and didn't deserve their careers. It means there's someone who just doesn't like them.

So, when you receive harsh words about your book-- whether they're from someone else or your own brain-- let it go. It's one book in a vast universe of books. It's one literary experience. At some point, you have to stop picking at it and just let it live the way it was intended.

That doesn't mean you have to completely tune out any and all feedback about the book. If something is universally confusing, then it might be in need of some patient tinkering. But if people just don't like it, then they can donate it or put it in a garage sale. Everyone in this world has albums, movies, books, and even clothing that they once loved, but now realize they bought in error. The world keeps turning.

Earlier in this book, I mentioned how you need to do some things for readers, such as make an intelligible book. That courtesy does not extend into making sure they absolutely adore the book. At the dawn of my career, I edited and beta read for a person whose books were truly appalling to me. I came to realize that I was just not the best beta reader for his books, and we parted ways amicably. Guess who's working with a team to develop his work for television. Everything has an audience. Don't find inspiration in the harsh words of the naysayers; grow with those who already know you're capable.

So, now that you've learned that you can always change things and no one's going to like everything anyway, including yourself, that leaves the question that started this chapter: How do you know when your book is done?

The very textbook, fact-based answer is that your book is done once you've reached a point where you're confident that it fully reflects all of the intentions you set forth in your pre-work. Though things changed during the pre-work and the writing itself, the general idea of writing a decent book on a specific topic should still be the bullseye you've been aiming for all along. If each page makes sense and contributes something to the overall book and reader experience, then you're done. Save the file. Submit. Print. Whatever you plan to do with your completed book, now is the time to do it. Have a toast, call your friends, cry… Whatever it takes to release all of the emotions and stress you've built along the way.

The esoteric version of this is that you'll simply know. Sometimes, you'll get through a round of edits and just know that your book is ready to fly. Alternatively, you'll be so sick of looking at it that you don't care if it flops, as long as it gets off of your desktop. Realistically, the logic behind these feelings is the knowledge within yourself that there is simply nothing else you can do to make the book any more ready than it is at that moment. But the romantic notion of understanding your book on a spiritual level is a bit more fun than really digging into the psychology of it.

If you are going to publish your book on a public level, beyond distribution to your inner circle, this is not the end of the line. You can certainly cheer, cry, and celebrate, but there may still be some work to be done on your end. Read on to determine how-- and if-- you want your book to see the light of day.

A Brief Word about Publishing

Years ago, publishing a piece meant sending it off to be printed in a bound book format with shiny covers and real pages that could be rudely dog-eared. With the advent of the household printer, it became easier to print off entire pieces without them ever passing the threshold, though it's difficult to say that using a household printer was ever "easy." Paper jams, impossible toner levels, and the cost of printer paper and ink made it a less than enjoyable process, but nonetheless, one anyone with the right equipment could complete.

Today, there are many paths to publication on a variety of scales. The difficulty, stress, and reward for each method are very different, and should be thoroughly considered before throwing all of your proverbial eggs into one proverbial basket.

Each of the methods for getting published that I'll mention is worthy of its own book, but I'm going to skim over each for now. There are several reasons for this. First, I don't want anyone to feel that publishing is mandatory. Writing for pleasure alone is still very much a real thing, and I want anyone attempting to write a book to feel like this can be our little secret. Next, the publishing world is so volatile that I couldn't possibly do it justice without writing a lengthy volume. Furthermore, the methods are constantly changing, and may be different from location to location, person to person, or website to website. It's a very nuanced business, so rather than provide you with any details that might be inaccurate, I'll instead give you the basics and point you in the direction of more authoritative information.

Ghost Writing

Ghost writing is a term used to describe a situation where one party hires another party to write about a particular topic on their behalf. Many people are looking for ghostwriters, especially those looking for someone to capture in written word their own advice or life story. As a new writer, this can be beneficial because someone else is giving you guidance, and that dangling paycheck just beyond the deadline can be a great incentive… as long as you're confident that you can follow through with the commitment.

Pros:
-    All you have to do is write and edit
-    No politics, no agents
-    You'll likely get paid
-    If the book tanks, no one knows it was you who wrote it

Cons:

- You usually do not get to choose the topic
- The person requesting the writing may have very specific requirements, including a deadline
- No commission
- If the book performs extremely well, no one knows it was you wrote it

Self Publishing

There are many venues out there for self-publishing your book, so take the time to explore your options to find the best fit for you and your goals. In this method of publication, you hire editors and designers to format your book, then submit it for publication through a business that strictly prints your book to order. Many publication venues have a minimum number of physical books they'll print at a time, but self published eBooks are extremely popular.

Pros:

- You can print anything, any time
- You don't have to print millions of copies
- You can earn commission, depending on the distribution method or site you use
- You can make changes to your book at any time, since they are printed to order. Just make sure you're using the latest file for future publications

Cons:

- You'll need to have design skills, or hire someone to ensure it's formatted correctly for publishing or ebook distribution
- You will not see your face smiling back at you from a book jacket in the window of a bookstore
- You don't commission unless it sells. All marketing and promotion is up to you
- You will need to pay for each copy that is produced, which means you may lose money at first

Finding an Agent/Publisher

This option is not for the faint of heart or those with low to moderate self-esteem. This is the most political version of getting your work published, but if you're very much interested in becoming a famous author, you'll want to consider finding an agent.

In this model, you send your book to agents who are looking for new material. Agents work on commission; therefore, it is in the best interest of each agent to only take on clients they believe they can sell. If an agent does not believe they can sell your book, they will reject it. Rejection hurts, but it's not personal.

Once you find an agent, the agent will pitch your book to a variety of publishing houses. Again, they will only accept your work if they think they can profit from it. If they don't think there's money in your book, they will reject it.

Eventually, your book will be published. You will be paid royalties which are a percentage of the profit on your book. Your book will need to sell a certain number of copies in order to pay for its own publishing, so you will only get paid after your book has "earned out," or paid for itself.

Pros:

- You don't have to pay to publish your own work
- You may be asked to produce multiple books
- Being signed by a publisher is a big deal with significant prestige and honor
- You won't have to do any of the hustling like marketing, printing, ordering, and design

Cons:

- You may have to relinquish creative control. Always review your contract in detail
- You may be rejected many times before you finally find an agent and publisher
- Your contract may limit your rights to your original work
- You may be forced to do press and signings (which might be a pro if you're into that sort of thing!)

Publishing your work is often a strange juxtaposition of guts and glory. I've included some resources to help you dig further into any and all options that might sound ideal for you and your goals for your freshly-written book.

Conclusion

So there you go. That's how you do it. Go write a book!

At this point, you may still feel like you don't entirely know "how" to write a book. I wish I could say that there's a step-by-step process that's super easy to follow and absolutely fail-proof, but there's really not.

Avid readers may recall the journey of a girl named Dorothy Gale along a certain Yellow Brick Road. She had guidance along the way, but there was quite a bit that she had to figure out on her own. At the risk of throwing yet another analogy on the heap, writing a book is a very similar exercise in endurance and perseverance. If you have a general idea of where you're headed and a destination or goal in mind, you'll be very well prepared to handle any bumps in the road that might head your way, whether you realize it or not.

You might feel right now that I haven't possibly addressed every single step, every possible problem or pratfall, and how to get out of it. In the most pragmatic way, you're quite right. But from a more internal, psychological standpoint, I have. Most of the obstacles that try us during the process of writing our first books come from the enemy within us. More than anything, novice writers are typically tripped up and dissuaded from completing big projects because they feel it would be a waste of time. They aren't good enough to write a book. They started a book once, but they lost interest in it. They decided they "sounded dumb," so they gave up. When I ask people how their books are going, and they clearly are not going well at all, these are the types of answers I receive.

What I hope I have impressed upon you, more than anything else, is that you have the power within you to get past these obstacles. Writing a book takes a lot of time, which is why I warned you of that right from the get go. Time, energy, and a sense of humor are all required in order to make it through the process of writing a book, whether it's your first or your 101st effort.

You will spend a lot of time writing a book, but whether that time is truly "wasted" is for you to decide. Human beings are very good at finding new and exciting ways to waste time, and frankly, if you felt like you got something from it emotionally, spiritually, mentally, physically, educationally, or what have you, then my personal view is that your time was not "wasted." It was used in an atypical way to provide you with personal enrichment.

As far as whether you're "good enough?" By now, you should be aware that we are all simultaneously good enough and not good enough. Some readers will love it. Some will hate it. The majority of readers will think it's fine and have no major feelings one way or another about it.

At the beginning of the book, we talked about maintaining realistic expectations for books and figuring out why we want to write them in the first place. Aligning our priorities mentally and emotionally when it comes to undertaking an entire tome is directly related to the level of energy we put into getting the task done. Aim higher than you need to, and you'll put undue pressure on yourself, struggling to write a book and ultimately feeling like you've "failed," which is false. You'll put too much energy in too fast and burn out when you discover the process can take a miserable amount of time and more than basic enthusiasm. As I've said, writing a bestseller is a remarkable goal, but don't register for the marathon without jogging a few steps first. You are good enough; you just need to set yourself up to succeed.

And then that sense of humor... At some point, everyone seems to feel like they "sound dumb." I would absolutely love to read more psychological and sociological studies examining why those in creative fields doubt their own abilities and intelligence. In the meantime, I can only speculate and recommend that you meditate on these concepts to see if they can help you break through some mental blockages of your own.

When you write, especially if you've never written before, you're using your mind and your body in new ways. It's all very unfamiliar, and sometimes, if you stare at a page or a word too long, you stop recognizing it. Don't let your brain play games with your spirit. A sense of humor will get you far in the writing process.

When you find yourself feeling ignorant or starting to have negative thoughts about your capabilities, take a break. Go do some research to validate yourself. Read a book from an author you admire. Some writers recommend reading an author in your genre, but I find that leads me down a path of temptation to compare myself to the other author. Let your brain find inspiration without dysfunction-- that is, fill your brain with information that will reignite your passion to pursue this endeavor, without feeding into any negative self-talk.

Always do the pre-work. As time goes by, and you gain more experience, you may find this part of the process going more and more smoothly. After a while, it starts to feel less like work and more like "the fun part." Really let yourself soar when it comes to dreaming up your book, especially in the very first few moments of making it real. Start really, really big, and then let yourself understand your book and where it really needs to go in order to make yourself clear.

In fact, allow yourself to suspend disbelief in your own reality a bit in these first few days of getting to know your book. I like to really immerse myself in whatever I'm writing about. If it's a particular brand of car, for example, I'll look at pictures, read the history of the manufacturer, even drive past a dealership lot if I can. When I'm writing a fiction piece, I like to really imagine who each character is. Don't give them arbitrary descriptions; instead, think about how they wear their hair (if they have hair). What's their posture like? How do they move? What do their facial expressions look like? It sounds a little strange at first, but consider how your belief in this new reality you're creating will help the reader ease more swiftly into your newfound world.

When you finally feel ready to sit down and write, make sure you are really prepared to commit to this undertaking. You're going to feel uncomfortable in every imaginable sense of the word, at least for the first few sessions. Are you prepared to break through the agony to pursue the ecstasies of writing?

Rather than arming you with a gimmick that claims to help newcomers write better, I'm furnishing you with certain truths and expectations that aren't discussed widely, though I'm not sure why the secrecy is so well-maintained. Whenever I mention through introduction that I'm a writer, this detail is more and more frequently met with a self-deprecating joke about how the other party is "practically illiterate," or something along those lines. While I would absolutely love to be validated in my suspicions that I am the most talented beast walking this planet, deep down inside I know that's not true.

Furthermore, it makes me very sad that so many people have had their confidence completely squelched when it comes to doing something creative. Why are standards so high that no one can simply dabble in art, music, crafting, cooking, or writing without being extremely good at it? You haven't "tried to write a book" if you got three sentences in and decided you were a failure. You weren't. You got overwhelmed. You psyched yourself out. You chose to quit before you became unbearably uncomfortable.

The writing process is truly unlike anything else. While there is some order to things, it's not an exact science, with the exception of some forms of nonfiction. If you prefer detailed instructions, you need to figure them out yourself. Just like the road trip from Seattle to Boca, there are a vast quantity of possible routes. But don't let that be your reason for never making the trip. Maps were made by people taking the trip and figuring out where to go. You'll need to make your own map the first time you make this particular journey, and that can certainly be overwhelming. But think how much more fun the next roadtrip will be, once you know the best route.

If you gain anything from this book, I want you to feel empowered by this to take the plunge and make it through the writing process. You certainly won't arrive at the end unscathed, but I hope that the previous pages have helped you understand some of the peril that awaits along the path. The creative process is all about exploration and experimentation, which can be utterly terrifying for those who have never dabbled in these particular areas. Take comfort in knowing that it doesn't go smoothly for anyone.

Press forward, and then press forward again. Dismiss criticism but consider constructive critique, even that which comes from your own mind.

For those who intend to distribute your book, keep in mind the benefits and things to be wary of when it comes to editing. Don't just worry about editors and beta readers, think about yourself and your relentless desire to pick things to bits *ad nauseum*. Learn when to make peace with, not pieces of, your book. Find a way to let go, and let it fly.

So how do you feel now? Ready to write a book? Take it one step at a time. When you get overwhelmed, pause yourself. Always maintain forward momentum. Don't get inside your own head.

And above all: Revel in every moment of the creative process. Even the not-so-lovely ones.

Good luck. May your fingers be swift and your muse always close at hand!

Resources

The following resources are intended to help inspire and excite you as a new writer. All sources have been credited where possible. Please don't consider the inclusion of any of these links as endorsements or partnerships; no one on the creative team is getting paid for sharing them, either. Consider this your friendly author friend sharing with you some interesting things that help them through this process.

The following sections outline all of the things you were promised in the main text and then some. I've included a variety of resources that will help you get out of sticky situations and guide you through some organization strategies, all with the goal of keeping that forward momentum and productivity rolling.

Enjoy at your own leisure, and remember, truly nothing in this world is beloved by all... not even cheese. I've made it a point to include a few different varieties of each resource, but if none of these suit your particular methods, use this as a launchpad for discovering your own way!

Writing Exercises

Writing truly is an exercise for the mind, spirit, and body. From time to time, you may find yourself lacking in whatever mojo gets the creative juices flowing. When this happens, consider a writing exercise or two to help you navigate back to a space where imagination is more possible and thoughts are more organized. I've included many different types of writing exercises, none of which are exclusively intended for writers of fiction or nonfiction. Basically, any time you find yourself falling off track, feel free to employ one of these exercises to help you find the way back to the path.

Eventually, you'll feel your flow return. If not, choose a different writing exercise, move on to brain cleansers, or grab a cup of tea and come back to it.

This is not a comprehensive list of exercises. These are just a few examples that I use in my own work. Feel free to look up even more exercises that will help your imagination soar.

1. <u>Narrate Your Day:</u> This one is fun because you don't even have to write anything down. This exercise is best in situations where you just can't get the words to appear, and you feel like you can't remember how to write.

To narrate your day, explain to yourself what you're doing at the moment. If you're a bit low on verbs, you can describe your surroundings. Don't think too much about it, just start describing:

"I sit perpendicular to a window. On my desk, which was once tragically painted white, a monitor glows bright white in the quickly dimming room."

"I was brushing my teeth. There was not enough toothpaste on the brush, but I lacked the concern to do anything about it. With my luck, I'd drop the toothbrush in the toilet if I tried to change anything about the situation. Best to let it ride."

Start with something obvious and real. Expand upon it. Add description. Give it life. Repeat.

2. <u>This Is My…</u>: *This* is another description exercise. I like to use this one when I'm trying to set a scene, bring a character to life, or really drive home a particular piece of evidence, but I seem to have forgotten all of my words.

For this exercise, choose an object. Any object, as long as you can actually see it and experience it in person at this exact moment. Start with the words, "This is my," followed by the name of the object. Then describe it. Don't worry about it making sense right away. Just start writing out your description, then keep going until you run out of things to say about it. Then keep going. Yes. Repeat yourself, then repeat yourself again. Eventually you will run out of things to say about your trinket or geejaw, but keep pushing yourself to say more, whether that means adding more adjectives and adverbs, or by including its significance in this universe.

"This is my lamp. It is pink. It is sitting on the upper left corner of my desk. I've had it for years. I don't know how many years. In fact, I forgot about it for a while. I found it in a box…" and so on.

3. <u>I Read the News Today, Oh Boy</u>: I like this one when I'm having trouble making connections happen or when I need to get over my own ego. You'll need some form of physical media that includes pictures and words such as a newspaper, magazine, brochure, or catalogue.

   Find a picture of a person. That's your protagonist. Find another picture of a person. That's your antagonist. Find a sentence that includes an action verb, like, "robbed a bank," or, "receives medal of honor." Write a little story in which those two people do those things. Remember this is just garbage, and write off the head. Excuse typos. Ignore grammar. Freestyle it. Feign shock and surprise when it turns out pretty good and becomes worthy of a little more effort and development, but finish one book before you start another.

4. <u>Get Out</u>: This is a bit of more traditional journaling, with a tad bit of therapy attached. Basically, you'll freewrite your way to mental freedom. Prepare a blank page. Close your eyes. Write. Every thought, make it come out. Think of it as clearing your cache.

Prompts

Many people use the terms "writing exercises" and "writing prompts" interchangeably. This isn't incorrect, but for the purpose of this book, I'm using "prompts" to describe mechanisms for getting unstuck when you've found yourself in a rut.

Use these prompts to help you redirect and refocus when you feel like you're repeating yourself, not saying enough, or "sound dumb". Reach out and grab onto these prompts like a carrot on a stick- they can help pull you to safety!

1. Select a specific person in your life and tell them what comes next. You can actually do this, or perform this exercise mentally. For example, "Ok, Meemaw, so after our hero goes to the castle, there's going to be a dragon, right? And the dragon is not going to see our hero, because... because... because he's under a sleeping spell!"

2. Stop acting like you're writing, and act like you're talking to someone. I strongly recommend you make a note to yourself in your writing journal about the exact page you were on when you implemented this prompt because things might get a little weird. Write exactly like you would speak, even if that includes curse words or colloquialisms, song lyrics, etc.. You will inevitably find yourself naturally "talking" your way back into the book's original format.

3. Look up synonyms. This may sound strange, but looking at words can sometimes reignite a mind that's been simmering on low for too long. I once submitted an article for publication thinking I'd done a good job. The editor asked me if I had realized I used the word "influence" ten times in a single paragraph and that two paragraphs covered the same information in different manners. My brain had clearly been stagnant. Looking up other words helped me diversify my thinking process and more forward meaningfully.

4. Ask yourself, "Why?". Children are very good at asking why things are the way they are, but adults tend to lose this sense of wonder. When you find yourself stumbling around, trying in vain to describe something or some piece of data, stop wandering and ask, "Why?"

   - Why did this happen?
   - Why do I need to know this?
   - Why am I explaining this now?
   - Why does the reader care?

Character Map Examples

For my fiction-writing friends, here are a few samples and templates to help you organize your characters. As discussed earlier, the purpose of a character map is to keep you from forgetting who is who and who does what. Additionally, a character map can help you discover more and more interesting traits regarding your characters. Each of these examples is quite different, so take a look, give each a try, and decide what you need to keep the citizens of your new world in line.

This particular form allows you to truly discover who your characters are as human beings. This is possibly the most detailed version I've found yet: http://www.epiguide.com/ep101/writing/charchart.html

Some of the ins and outs of character mapping techniques, along with great examples:

https://www.thenovelry.com/blog/character-map

Here's a technique that involves a family-tree style map, as well as tips on organizing their biographies:

http://writeonsisters.com/writing-craft/6-easy-steps-to-great-character-mapping/

This link leads to an online shop for teachers to share and sell character map templates. The prices are quite reasonable, especially for a resource you'll enjoy many times over!

https://www.teacherspayteachers.com/Browse/Search:character%20map%20template

Plot Outline Examples

If you do a simple search for "plot outlines" or "plot diagrams,"you'll more than likely find a drawing of a line that rises slowly, reaches a peak, then plummets swiftly. This drawing is the simplest explanation of a plot. As a writer, you'll find that your plot greatly resembles a distressed spider's web rather than a beautiful single line. At the same time, sometimes the simplest templates get the job done. Here are a few examples of plot outlines to help you get your own plot details situated. This is an example of someone's personal template, and I very much like the style and simplicity of it. If you're in the early stages of figuring out actions and reactions, give a sample like this a try.

https://karcherry.files.wordpress.com/2013/07/plot-outline1.jpg

This version is very handy for those who have multiple questions to answer through the course of their book. Very rarely is our hero focused on just one thing at a time. An outline like this will help you reveal and map the course of each source of strife.

https://diymfa.com/writing/mapping-out-your-story

This link leads to several different types of plot outline templates. I like #5 in particular, because it looks a lot like my own plot outlines. If you're not sure which version of a plot outline would best stimulate your brain, take a cruise through the examples here to try a few different options.

https://templatelab.com/story-outline/

And since we've used her works as an example several times, I thought it might be interesting to share with you how author J.K. Rowling put together the *Harry Potter* books. This article includes the handwritten plot outline for chapters 13–24 of *Harry Potter and the Order of the Phoenix*. Notice how she tracks all of the simultaneously existing storylines on the horizontal, then fills in the necessary developments to each story on the vertical, chapter by chapter.

http://blog.paperblanks.com/2013/05/j-k-rowling-book-outline/

Nonfiction works also require significant pre-work, as we discovered in the second section of this book. The purpose of an outline is to help you figure out how to get from one important point in your discussion to another. You can use the outline to help you set the tone, or to help you remember key resources or quotes to help drive your discourse forward.

In the interest of showing my own work, here's my own outline for this book. Basically, I started with the concept of "How to Write a Book." Then, I quite literally went stream of consciousness for the outline so that I could nail down what I wanted to share. I'm sure you'll be able to spot the differences and similarities.

https://docs.google.com/document/d/1Pbv1obA4W_v_IlQYRMHP-8VArTHyj-upb94CW1dq2474/edit?usp=sharing

As you can see, my method most reflects the standard outline method presented here.

https://writenonfictionnow.com/outlining-first-time-self-published-authors/

One extra tidbit I'd like to add is that, if you are using quotes or specific sections of resources, it is very helpful to include a link or the basic bibliographic information for that quote or resource in your outline so you don't struggle to find it later.

Here is the world-famous Scrivener outline method. This writer provides a video as well as an explanation as to how the method works for her and some tips and tricks for using it.

https://authorbasics.com/using-scrivener-outline-non-fiction-book/

There are a few different samples included in this link for different types of nonfiction. If you're writing a book that isn't a simple wander through the points to be made and discussions to be had, this link will help you figure out a creative and enjoyable flow of thoughts for your audience.

https://laptrinhx.com/news/how-to-write-a-nonfiction-book-free-chapter-outlining-templates-oAZ8D5e/

Nonfiction Table Of Contents Examples

My editors will be the first people to tell you that my inclusion of this topic is purely hypocritical, since I really don't follow any particular format or template when I'm writing for myself. I abandoned the idea of following a format during my first year of copywriting. I discovered that every client had developed their own formatting, and it's best to forget what you were taught in school and do what the person with the money wants. However, as a new writer who has not been subjected to years of memorizing the nuances of various formats only to have them change before you can put them to use, you likely would like some help with formatting.

The following are sites that provide templates for creating a TOC for your nonfiction masterpiece.

This link includes a variety of formats and templates, ranging from the highly stylistic to the very structured. Remember that you are using the TOC to help you organize and stay on track, and choose a version that is right for the task.

https://www.template.net/business/word-templates/table-of-contents/

I like this guide from Sam Houston University (again, I have no affiliation with them; I simply like the link) because it demonstrates the full scholarly version of the table of contents, which you will note I personally have completely disregarded. If you are going to be shopping your work to a publisher, you'll most likely need to write this more formal APA version of a table of contents in your final draft before shipping it off...

https://shsulibraryguides.org/thesisguide/tableofcontents

...unless you're using the Chicago style, in which case, you'll want to click on this link, instead.

https://www.scientific-editing.info/blog/chicago-table-of-contents/

If you just saw the words "APA" and "Chicago" in the section above and had a mild wave of anxiety pass over you because you don't know what those are, here's an explanation. As mentioned in the chapter regarding the organization or format of your piece, there are quite a few different methods, none of which are super important unless you're looking to publish your piece or place it under formal review. Again, I'm a very naughty writer who has used a mish-mash of styles for this book, but it's pretty clear by now that this is a very casual, candid piece and not a scholarly work.

Check out the following links and decide which feels more natural for you. If you are submitting your work for publishing or review, double check with the publisher regarding their exact formatting requirements.

APA: American Psychological Association. Yes, really. Their preferred publishing format has been adopted across the writing community for scholarly pieces.
https://apastyle.apa.org/

Chicago: Developed in 1906 by the University of Chicago Press, this style is usually associated with topics surrounding business, arts, history, and humanities.
https://www.chicagomanualofstyle.org/home.html

MLA: The Modern Language Association developed this format in 1833, and it's changed several times since then. Currently in their 9th edition, MLA sells handbooks, though some rules and tips are provided free of charge online. This style is generally applied to studies of language, culture, and human interest, and is very popular with college professors.

https://style.mla.org/mla-format

MECE (Mutually Exclusive, Collectively Exhaustive): This is not a publication format, but rather an organizational formatting option. It's somewhat controversial; however, for those who have a tendency to go off on stream of consciousness tangents when writing, it can help provide a little discipline when organizing your nonfiction piece.

https://www.caseinterview.com/mece

Desk Exercises

Writing is hard on the body as well as the mind, especially if you're not used to sitting down and wiggling your fingers to make words appear for hours at a time. You may find your back, posterior, legs, hips, arms, and fingers aching after your first few sessions.

Additionally, a stagnant body can lead to a bored mind, which is not helpful when you're trying to be creative. Get up and move every 30 minutes or so, or when you find yourself at a loss for words.

In reading these links, please note that I am not a doctor, and nothing I write should be considered medical advice. Always address discomfort with a trained physician.

This link offers loads of exercises you can do without leaving your desk, though you should definitely leave your desk every once in a while!
https://www.healthline.com/health/fitness/office-exercises

You're going to have to get up from your desk to do these exercises, but you'll be glad you did:
https://yogawithadriene.com/yoga-for-writers/

Here are some hand and wrist exercises to help you keep limber in between sessions:
https://www.webmd.com/osteoarthritis/ss/slideshow-hand-finger-exercises

This link provides some excellent options for getting your cardio in while being psychologically chained to your writing. Plus, it uses the term "Deskercise," which I adore.
https://greatist.com/fitness/deskercise-33-ways-exercise-work

Brain Cleansers

Brain cleansers are exercises for your mind and emotions. Writing can be draining, especially if you're very passionate about what you're writing or are simply feeling stressed by any part of the process. Stress is normal and can be good, but too much leads to writer's block, headaches, or worse-- quitting.

If you feel yourself getting overwhelmed, here are a few things you can do to chill out and get back on task:

Yoga Nidra:
Yoga Nidra is an excellent relaxation and centering technique that allows you to bring awareness to each part of your body individually. It's a form of meditation that can not only reorganize a frazzled brain, it can also bring your brain into a state of restfulness without that post-nap grogginess.

I don't know this person or have any affiliation with their YouTube channel, but I do appreciate the variety of practices offered here: https://www.youtube.com/c/SarovaraYoga

For those who would like to learn more about the practice, a colleague of mine has written a book on the topic that gives a great introduction. I do know this person, but I'm not getting any kickbacks for mentioning her book:

https://www.amazon.com/Nidra-Yoga-beginners-increase-productivity-ebook/dp/B07ZQR81PT/ref=tmm_kin_swatch_0?_encoding=UTF8&qid=1635527242&sr=8-1

Games:

Depending on where your stress levels have taken you, you might prefer playing a game to help you return to your regular functional self. These games have been recommended for those looking to tune back into themselves and leave the chaos behind:

https://www.self.com/story/free-mobile-games

These, on the other hand, will spark greater activity in the brain:

https://www.lifehack.org/articles/technology/11-brain-training-apps-train-your-mind-and-improve-memory.html

Breathing Exercises:

You may not connect breathing with your brain, but when the thoughts stop and your heart starts racing, focusing on your breathing can restore harmony in your body.

https://www.uofmhealth.org/health-library/uz2255

https://www.youtube.com/watch?v=MlaSf1DgtbA

https://yogawithadriene.com/free-yoga-videos/pranayama/

Since I glossed over this topic earlier, I've included a few helpful resources to help guide you further along with the various publication options mentioned earlier.

Ghostwriting:

The steps and tricks you'll need to keep in mind when getting started as a ghostwriter:
https://thewritelife.com/how-to-become-a-ghostwriter/

Some things to consider before you take the plunge:
https://theregalwriter.com/2020/10/09/know-the-pros-and-cons-of-ghostwriting/

Self-publishing:

Where you can go to get your book self published:
https://selfpublishing.com/self-publishing-companies/

Amazon's guide to self-publishing:
https://kdp.amazon.com/en_US/

How to get started with the process, and knowing whether it's ideal for you:

https://knliterary.com/how-to-self-publish-a-book/

Traditional publishing:

This guide provides very detailed and solid information on both self and traditional publishing:

https://writersdigestshop.com/pages/how-to-publish-a-book-an-overview-of-traditional-self-publishing

This guide includes real authors talking about the process and the various considerations of traditional publishing:

https://getpublished.penguin.co.uk/

This article includes links to some common resources for finding and wooing a literary agent:

https://shutupwrite.com/how-to-find-a-literary-agent/

Communities for New Writers

For those looking for support, encouragement, critique, or validation, here are some links to online forums or communities dedicated to new writers. I cannot speak for the overall quality or politeness of all communities, so I encourage you to read and lurk a bit before you start joining in the discussion. Like all groups of people, some will be ideal for you and others will not. Proceed at your own risk.

Writing Forums: https://www.writingforums.com/

She Writes: https://www.shewrites.com/

NaNoWriMo: https://nanowrimo.org/

Critique Circle: https://new.critiquecircle.com/landing

Go forth, be bold, and write a book!

ONE WORD
AT A TIME

How to Write a Fiction Book for Beginners

Lauren Bingham

Introduction

How does one start an instructional book about writing fiction?

On one hand, you want to encourage your audience that writing a fiction book is a splendid idea which they should pursue. I have every urge to be your cheerleader and best supporter and tell everyone that it's a fantastic idea that they surely won't regret.

At the same time, there's the "cautious parent" aspect of the enterprise. "It's not easy," I want to gently warn people. "It's going to be difficult. You'll get frustrated. It's enough to make a preacher cuss." But, in my experience, admonitions are the opposite of inspiration. I don't want to scare potential award-winning writers off the trail with cursing clergy.

It is my years of experience in writing that tells me that both of these instincts are equally valid and useful to the up-and-coming author. You should be excited, and I'm excited for you. You should also be terrified, and I'm here to hold your hand and get you through it.

If you read the first book in this series, *How to Write a Book: A Book for Anyone Who Has Never Written a Book (But Wants To),* you got a taste of how to get motivated and remain optimistic as you traipse through your first attempt at writing a book. Rather than sternly remind you not to mix up your gerund and participle phrases (because I'm equally guilty), the first book took an emotional support role to the creative process. We strolled through the possibilities of fiction and nonfiction alike to determine how to step off the platform of indecision and ride the train of writing your first book.

This book is for my fellow fiction writers. I realize that this particular book is a work of nonfiction, but rest assured that I have spent my fair share of time daydreaming plot twists and characters with the best of them. There's something so completely fascinating about the notion of being encouraged to create an entirely imaginary world, full of people who will never exist, doing things that have never happened in the sequence portrayed... or have they?

Fiction writing is not for everyone. "It's complicated" feels like the most laughably simple way to describe all of the things happening at once inside the brain of a fiction writer. You've got characters, right? And they're all doing things, so you've got to figure out who is doing what and when. Then, you've got to keep all the characters organized, not only by what they're doing, but how they do it, who they are, and why they're doing what they're doing.

But, you can't just plod on with page after page of "and then they… and then they… and then they," either. You need a compelling plot, one that simultaneously teaches, entertains, amazes, and touches people in a meaningful way. You're not just writing your heart out; you're writing personally to the mind and soul of every person who might be impacted by your prose.

People read fiction because they want to be impacted. They want to have complicated emotions about your characters. They want to frantically devour each page, racing towards the end, and yet not wanting to reach it, because "The End" signifies the outer limits of the world shared by characters and reader alike. That means devising ways to welcome them into your world and to keep them on a wondrous path at all times.

If the magnitude of the responsibility carried by fiction writers seems more than you can manage, that doesn't mean you should immediately return this book for a refund. Instead, it means you go ahead and write anyway because writing for yourself is just as important as writing for a major award.

People read fiction for the impact. People write fiction because they want to. No one is forced to write fiction. In fact, I will never personally know if you never write anything more than a witty tweet. You likely picked up this book and started reading because the subject interested you, which means at some point in your life, you've wondered what is involved in writing a piece of fiction and how it's done. Maybe you also wondered if you were the type of person who could do it.

Have you ever gotten caught staring at a stranger on the train, and wanted to explain, "No, no– I'm not a creep. I actually just thought that my protagonist would really like your haircut?" Or have you ever entered a place so phenomenal that you immediately started a narrative description of it, either out loud or to yourself? Do you happen to add more adjectives and adverbs to your emails and conversations than the average human?

If you answered "yes" or "maybe" to any of these questions, you might be a fiction writer. And if you might be a fiction writer, but you're not entirely certain, this book is for you.

Will this book make up your mind for you, drive you to your desk, adhere you to your keyboard, and force the most exquisite prose to flow freely from your fingertips? No, but I wish it would because I could benefit from that as well.

Instead, this book is going to take you on a behind-the-scenes tour of the world of fiction. Much as a tour guide points out things you should be looking at as you stroll through a museum or roll through a safari, this book is going to ask you to look at certain elements of what constitutes great fiction.

Though I love the idea of having ultimate control, I am relinquishing a lot of the duty of choosing words and conjugating verbs to you. I'm not going to tell you what to do or how to do it. Instead, I'm going to share with you some of the key elements of a successful story, and then we're going to practice it together. And by "practice," I mean "writing exercises."

Don't start groaning yet! Personally, I find writing exercises fun. For a ten minute period of my life, I can plop whatever gibberish comes rolling off my fingers onto a page and exorcize the demons of writer's block and formatting while exercising my muses. There is a notion in the writing world that these little exercises, which at the time look like junk on a page, can grow and blossom into fantastic work. I am here to confirm that this is true. Some of my favorite pieces have taken seed as something as simple as a phrase I used in a writing exercise.

However, I recognize that some people are not at that same stage of enthusiasm for extra work. I can't encourage you to be happy about the assignments, but I encourage you to at least think about the topic, and how you could go about it. If it's possible to extract an entire story out of a small turn of phrase, imagine the disservice you would be doing yourself if you kept that story all locked up in your mind just because you didn't want to do ten minutes of brainstorming!

You don't have to do all of the exercises in this book, and as I mentioned earlier, I'll never know whether you did or not. But, to entice and encourage you to make this an interactive experience, I'm going to be doing each of the exercises along with you. It is, after all, a behind-the-scenes tour. I'll show you exactly what I wrote for these prompts. I'll also take a few opportunities to show you how I got from what I considered junk to something I would submit for publishing through the power of reading, re-reading, and carefully editing.

For all intents and purposes, you are prepared to write a story right now. All you really have to do is type. But, if you're looking for that extra mile of guidance, the support to know you are "doing it right," and to help you figure out how to get from "once upon a time" to "the end," I am looking forward to taking this journey with you. Together, we'll take your ideas, sort them out, make them pretty, and create a story you'll want to share time and time again.

My goal is to make this book enjoyable for everyone, no matter how loosely formed or tightly wound your interest in writing fiction is at this exact moment. Therefore, we'll take a look at what I consider the key elements of creating decent fiction. We'll start with a look at the planning stage, and how an inkling of an idea becomes a fully-drawn outline. Then we'll dive into character, plot, and dialogue. We'll try a variety of exercises that demonstrate how every word you use matters, whether it sets the tone, builds action, or provides insight into the people, places, and things that make your story unique.

At the end of many of the chapters, you'll find a writing exercise. First, I'll describe the exercise and provide guidelines for you to complete it on your own. You won't need any special equipment– just a ten minute timer and your favorite writing implements. Feel free to use manual writing materials such as pen and paper or quill and vellum, or those of the digital variety, such as a laptop or tablet. And, as I mentioned before, if the spirit doesn't move you to do the exercises right this second, at least give yourself ten minutes to think about the prompt and how you would go about completing the exercise.

I'll also share what happened when I tried the prompt. In some instances, I'll even show you various versions and rewrites of my efforts, so you can see how applying different lenses, voices, and theories to your work can change how it reads without changing the meaning. It might sound confusing now, but there will be plenty of examples along the way.

We'll wrap things up with a look at the editing process. Again, we won't be drilling down to the technical level, but we'll look at how words are important to the writing process, and how what you say– or don't say– can make the art of fiction that much more fantastic.

Writing your first piece of fiction will still take work, and there still may be a full range of emotions involved in the process. However, my goal with this book is to demonstrate that it can be fun and enjoyable and that putting the pieces together to make a lovely little story is ultimately rewarding. In fact, many people enjoy it so much that they find themselves doing it again and again. We call those people "writers."

So, if you're ready to take that first step towards becoming a writer in your own right, let's get started!

What Makes Fiction, Fiction

When I was in college, I was faced with a terrible choice. I had exactly 72 hours to choose between majoring in Creative Writing or Anthropology. This happened at the beginning of the term, and I hadn't even attended some of my classes yet.

So, there I was, a fresh-faced and irresponsible 18-year-old, mulling over this important decision that would impact the rest of my life. Then, I was asked yet another question that I was not prepared to answer. Looming over my desk, my British Literature professor peered over the mighty depths of his glasses and asked, "Miss Bingham, what is fiction?"

As a person who rarely spoke in public at the time, my first reaction was to turn beet red while my lips glued themselves together. I looked up, sweat beading on my hairline, and said, "It's a story that isn't true."

And the professor, in the uncanny nature of professors around the world who have caught their students in an incomplete answer replied, "Yes, but many of the things we see on the internet aren't true. What makes fiction, fiction?"

Mercifully, he stepped away and engaged the rest of the class in a robust discussion about what constitutes fiction. Is an imaginary friend considered fiction? When you think ahead about the bad things that could happen if you follow this path or that path instead, is that fiction? Are poorly researched news stories where journalists insert details that they have invented or assume to be true also fiction?

Ultimately, we stumbled up on the overall definition the professor was attempting to coax from us. Fiction is a type of story-telling. In this story, there are characters. The characters interact with each other and their environment. These characters do things, and the things they do tell us about who they are. Their wants and needs motivate them to make changes. The things they do, and the consequences of doing them are the plot.

The premise of fiction is that the details are make-believe. The characters are imaginary people doing hypothetical things in a land that does not exist. That being said, many fictional pieces are based very much on real people, events, and places. Take, for example, films such as *Titanic* or *Amadeus*. Both include very healthy doses of reality, but are overall fictionalized accounts of people or situations that occurred.

The point of fiction is to make us think about our own humanity, to experience emotions, to feel empathy, and to share an adventure with people we only meet on pages in far away places we've never visited.

Therefore, fiction is much more than my desperate response of "a story that isn't true." Whether anything in the story has its base in reality, or is completely the invention of the author, fiction matters to people because it takes us places and makes us feel things. As long as the words stream along the pages, the reader is standing right beside the characters, observing everything they see and hearing their every thought. Despite the fact that readers and writers don't always get the chance to meet outside the pages of a story, the experience of reading a great piece of fiction brings people together.

From the basis of understanding what fiction is, we can then start to classify the types of fiction. Depending on who you ask, there are anywhere from 5 to 144 genres, or types of fiction. Don't let this confuse you. Literature is, after all, a creative process, just like visual art and music. Each author has their own nuances, and the themes they explore in each piece might travel the line between genres.

Some of the more popular versions that you might encounter in a local bookstore or library include:

- Science Fiction
- Fantasy
- Mystery
- Thriller
- Western
- Romance
- Young Adult
- Historical Fiction

It is not unheard of to cross genres a bit. J.K. Rowling's *Harry Potter* series, for example, is intended for young adults and includes strong elements of fantasy and a little romance tossed in there as well. Author Neil Gaiman also weaves tales that are part fable, based in religious elements, take a few turns into horror, and blend science fiction and fantasy in such a way that readers are fully willing to suspend disbelief... Many of his works can be found in the young adult section as well. Chuck Palahniuk describes his work as "transgressional fiction," which is certainly an accurate representation of his hyper-realistic yet fantastical explorations of the human psyche and the frailty within.

Many first-time writers get caught up in the web of over-thinking their first literary endeavors. I encourage you to not subscribe too enthusiastically to the concepts of genre and "rules" when you're first stretching your creative muscles. Instead, let yourself explore the ideas and concepts that come to mind. Let the creativity flow and allow inspiration to take you on a magical voyage as you put words on the page.

Frankly, the idea of "rules" in a creative process seems a little inappropriate. Innovation is essentially the destruction of regulations. However, if you're the type of person who craves structure, it's certainly not outside the realm of possibility to adopt the framework typically associated with a particular genre.

For example, books that fall under the fantasy category have a few unified elements. Magic and magical systems are often central to the story. This doesn't necessarily have to take the form of magic wands and spells, but instead refers to anything that flies in the face of our current understanding of physics. Characters who can fly, teleport, shape shift, or become invisible are all examples of magical elements.

Fantasy books also tend to have a well-developed sense of setting. Since these stories require readers to believe entirely in things that are very much not real, establishing as much "reality" as possible will help them suspend disbelief and fully immerse themselves in the world you have created.

You'll frequently find a theme of a corrupt and all-powerful government in fantasy works, along with a well-established sense of "good" and "evil." This government and its policies generally set up the basis for the conflict that creates the rising action of the tale, and frequently culminates in a battle between the sides.

But what if you want to write a book about unicorns who wear cowboy hats and heartily lust over each other from across the meadows? Is that a fantasy, a western, or a romance?

Questions and grey areas such as these are exactly why I encourage those who are new to writing not to fuss too much with the rules and guidelines of any one particular genre of fiction. If you need pointers such as those previously outlined for fantasy books, by all means incorporate them into the planning stages of your piece. But for those who just want to write without overthinking it, I encourage you to do exactly that: just write. Put words on the page and come back later to fuss over the technicalities. And if that concept sounds absolutely terrifying, fear not– we're going to be doing exactly that through the course of this book. If you follow along with all of the exercises, you'll be well-seasoned in putting words on a page by the time we get to the section about editing.

Many writers question and second-guess themselves when it comes to preparing for their first time out of the literary gate. This is a natural part of the process, even for those of us who are well-seasoned. Some people hypothesize that this intense level of self-doubt is responsible for burgeoning substance abuse issues among those in creative fields, and there might be something to that. However, you don't have to get completely plastered to write a quality piece of fiction. Just ignore your brain and write. Close your eyes if you need to. Let the process happen, and fix things up later. After all, you don't paint the walls and set up your furniture in a house you haven't built yet. Just write!

With all of this in mind, it's time to get started with the planning phase of your first fiction piece.

The Planning Stage

Given what I just said about "putting words on the page," the idea of a "planning stage" may seem counter-intuitive.

In *How to Write a Book: A Book for Anyone Who Has Never Written a Book (But Wants To),* we cover creating a character map and a plot outline. Each of these can be very helpful in getting your thoughts together and organizing finer details so you don't essentially write yourself into a corner. I encourage you to do both, or either, depending on your level of comfort and experience with writing.

The character map allows you to outline the "who's who" of your characters, as well as connect the dots between them to establish relationships. Similarly, the plot map helps you establish what happens in the rising action that leads to the climax of the tale, and then sort out what needs to be covered in the falling action, or denouement.

For the sake of creating a truly immersive experience in fiction, let's take a step back from those practical pieces of the planning stage, and focus on the point of inception. A story begins with a thought, an idea, a character, or a simple turn of phrase that you find inspiring. But, forming that thought into a full-fledged story will take a little finesse. Let's take a trip through the process of turning this glimmer of inspiration into a realizable dream.

Chapter 1 : What Is Your Story About?

This world is filled with few guarantees, but it seems like any time you divulge to others that you've got this great idea for a book, they will immediately ask, "Oh really? What's your story about?"

Honest answers to this question are always a little messy. For example, the fiction piece I submitted for my thesis was described by the reviewing committee as, "...a series of short stories surrounding a variety of characters in the LGBTQA+ community of a large city and the lessons they learn about themselves and society." That's a pretty neat and tidy way to wrap it up, but it really doesn't reveal the colorful tapestry of drag queens, underground raves, sexual mores, social responsibility, substance abuse, mental health, friendship, and love that really make the story move along. When describing it to my staff advisor, I actually described it as, "*Winesburg, Ohio*, only written by someone who has read too much Oscar Wilde and James Joyce." He obviously cringed at the prospect of slugging through this proposal, but ultimately, the committee loved it.

Don't be afraid to be messy when it comes to describing what your book is about. In fact, the messier you get, the more interesting possibilities you'll uncover. Nearly every professional writer has found themselves truly surprised by how things shake out once they've started really planning their book.

But, how do you get started deciding what your book is *really* about? Personally, I recommend creating a document, journal, giant chalkboard, or other space in which you can brainstorm or idea-dump at will. Jot down every single idea you have about your story as it comes to you. Think of your brain as a jar full of sand in which you can find a single diamond. You could try carefully extracting the diamond without disturbing the sand by picking around or using tweezers, or you could dump out all of the contents and sift through them until you've found the prize.

Jotting down every idea is a similar process. It can and will get messy, but from the mess you'll be able to pick out all the diamonds that will make your story shine.

As an example of how this can work, let's take a look at the brainstorming/idea dumping process I went through for a short story I recently wrote. This short story actually came about while I was working on a writing exercise, and I'll show you what came out of that exercise later in this book and how it continued through the development process.

The essence of the exercise is about following a character's train of thought in an unlikely situation- it's called "The Unexpected Guest," and you can feel free to jump ahead to this exercise if you can't wait to try it out yourself. Just bear in mind that your results at this stage in the process will be a bit different than what you might write after we discuss the planning stage in whole.

For my "unexpected guest," I decided to have my point of view character meet her teenage celebrity crush on an airplane. After I completed the ten minute exercise, I realized this could be a really fun short story. Synch the action up with the duration of the flight, and I could be sitting on a witty little tale.

Here are the notes I made after the writing exercise before attempting to turn it into a short story:

Passenger: Female, age 42. Name? Professional- successful. Thinks she's more awkward than she really is. Introvert.

Crush: Jason Ergway, late 50s/early 60s? Older. Former rock star. Middle school dance necking stuff. Has aged well. Think Richard Marx, not Rex Manning.

Flight: Short. Baltimore to Raleigh? Across Texas? Cities, but not super popular. Short flight, but still long enough to have drink service. He's not doing publicity. He's just being a person in a plane going somewhere. Early in the morning. Too early. Emotions are high and everyone is cranky. How did Passenger end up in First Class?

Where is Passenger going and why?

She is stressed and upset. Is that about travel or has to do with destination/reason for traveling?

Does anyone else recognize JE? Stewardess does not. She is too young. No one else saw him pre-board. Is Passenger daydreaming? Is this real life?

Interaction: JE is polite but not interested in talking much. Passenger is shy and sweaty. Very awkward.

Catalyst to conversation: Is JE in her seat? Does he ask to get up too often? What will make this extra awkward?

Give it a happy ending. JE and Passenger don't need to hook up, but maybe they find common ground. Job offer? Mutual friends? Let's have them keep in touch somehow. Happy Memory.

As you can see, there were still a lot of questions in the first stages of deciding what my story is about. That's because I honestly didn't know what I had and where I was going.

Please do yourself a favor and start here. Then keep going. Start answering the questions. And if a question is too much, keep going and see if you can go back and answer it later.

With this particular piece, I was really stuck on the "is this really happening/is this a fantasy" bit. But I knew in my heart of hearts (and from past experience) that if I let myself really overthink that question, I was going to devote all of my energy towards working through that problem and become exhausted with this piece before I could finish it.

Therefore, if you find yourself getting stuck on a question at this stage, simply let it stick there. Walk around it, leave it in the rearview, and keep going. You don't have to know how your story is going to end in order to start the writing process. You just need to have a good idea of what your story is about.

Chapter 2 : Who Is in It?

Try to imagine a story without characters. Not even a narrator, or a second-person point of view. No one at all.

It doesn't work very well, does it? In order to have things happen, someone or something has to be doing it– even you (implied). Even if the narrative is from the point of view of something inanimate, like the wind describing how it blows, or a leaf bemoaning its journey to the ground, there is still a noun, verbing.

At the same time, characters are much more than just doers of all the things. Characters are not flat, represented by a name or describable attribute. Rather, they are multi-dimensional representations of actual humanity... or whatever life form your characters may take.

I hesitate to call characters "humans" or "people" because they don't necessarily have to be *Homo sapiens*. Instead, they could be animals, the features of a landscape, your furniture, or the items in your junk drawer. I've edited stories told from the point of view of a crayon, a cloud, a child's diary, and even a vacuum cleaner. However bizarre the identity of the characters, they were unified in one aspect : they were clearly defined and described.

At this stage in the writing process, I encourage you to not get hung up on the full description of your characters. In fact, in just a few chapters, we'll do a few exercises together that will help you focus on bringing your characters to life.

In the planning stage, keep things simple. As you can see from my example, we don't even know the point of view character's name yet. Things like hair color, race, clothing style, or other visual identifiers are nowhere in sight. Instead, I mentioned things I already knew, such as the ages of the characters.

If your characters have formally introduced themselves to you, by all means include what they've shared about themselves. However, if you only know that the main characters are a teenage boy and his mother, leave it there for now. When you build a house, you don't put up a fully wallpapered living room before you pour the base or construct the frame, and that's exactly what we're doing in the planning stage.

That doesn't mean that we dismiss any wallpaper swatches that might come to our attention. We save these details as possibilities–inspiration for what could be, and even what absolutely must be. In some cases, the swatches can change. The character you originally planned to be a middle-aged woman becomes an octogenarian man, or the rabbit turns out to be a skunk. Other times, it is absolutely essential that the main character take a specific image, just as you need to consider the footprint of your basement before you nail the shingles to your roof. I encourage you to write down whatever details you have in mind at the time of your planning session, but don't strain yourself to come up with intimate details. We'll do that later.

You'll also want to have an overall idea of what your characters are going to do. You may not know exactly when or how these events are going to unfold, but you should have an idea of what needs to happen to make your story complete. You are certain that the kids from Derry, Maine are going to face off against "It." You know that Katniss Everdeen is going to participate in the Hunger Games. You have no doubt that Robert Langdon is going to crack the next step in an ancient code just moments before the bad guys figure it out.

Many of us have a natural, instinctual desire to want to figure everything out right away. One of the hardest parts of the writing process for newcomers is realizing that you're not going to be able to figure it out right away. Consider Dorothy in L. Frank Baum's *The Wizard of Oz*. She's advised that she'll have to travel the yellow brick road in order to consult the Wizard regarding her return trip to Kansas. She has absolutely no idea where this road leads and little indication as to how the Wizard will help, or who he really is.

This is a fantastic metaphor for where you are in the writing process in the planning stages. You've got a path to follow, even though it's completely unfamiliar and everyone is being strangely coy about what you'll encounter between here and your destination. You know that you need to meet the Wizard at the end, whoever they may be. Oh yes, and there's an evil witch buzzing around your head, trying to get revenge on you for killing her sister. In the writing world, we call that witch "deadlines." Don't worry about her just yet. Just keep typing your way down the yellow brick road. You'll find your way to the Wizard at the end, and he'll have all the answers.

Chapter 3 : When and Where Does It Take Place?

The setting of your story can be minutely specific, or vastly broad. You can visit many places through the course of your story, or everything can happen without the characters leaving the spot where we met them.

In the example I shared, our characters were settling in on an airplane. As my notes indicated, they're going to be taking a short regional flight from one city to another. There are other important notes about the setting as well. I specifically mention that this is an early morning flight.

But why? What do these elements of setting actually mean for the story itself? Why does it matter if the flight is at 6am or 6pm? Who cares how long the flight is, or where it's going?

The when and where of your story can have a major impact on what's happening and your characters' motivation for doing the things they do. From the physical plane of existence to the thoughts and emotions your characters are processing throughout your story, setting is a serious factor.

Writers live by the theory "show; don't tell," so let's try a little starter exercise to allow me to demonstrate what kind of an impact the when and where can have on your story.

. . . .

Exercise Alert! Planning Your Setting

Let's try a little practice exercise to demonstrate this concept. You don't have to write this one down, but you are welcome to do so. Consider this an informal "warm up."

Pick one of these scenarios:
1.   You are comfy and cozy.
2.   You are about to eat the best meal ever.
3.   Your shoelace broke.

Each of these is a pretty vague prompt. You probably have a few questions about what happens next, or why it matters. That's exactly what I want you to write or think about for this exercise.

For the scenario you've chosen, I want you to answer the question, "Where?" Give yourself five minutes to jot down some ideas, or contemplate where these things are happening. As you can see, I eliminated the need for creating characters by making you the narrator here. Therefore, from your very own point of view, I want you to tell your readers where *you* are when you're comfy and cozy, about to eat the best meal ever, or when your shoelace broke.

Don't worry about using complete sentences, or coming up with anything you'd ever put in a manuscript. Once you've got five minutes of consideration behind this exercise, come back to this text, and we'll talk about what happened.

....

Ready to move forward with the results of your exercise?

First, here's what I came up with:

My shoelace broke at the store. It's 7.30am, and I'm trying to buy some stuff to cobble together some kind of crappy lunch, and my stupid shoelace broke. I don't even know what I want for lunch, but now I have to act like I didn't just almost fall out of my shoe rounding the corner into the lunch meat aisle. I don't even like lunch meat. Why am I even here? I should have just gone to the office and made coffee and sucked it up and paid $10 for stupid delivery. But oh no, stupid me with her worn out stupid shoelaces had to come to the only open mega mart store ten minutes before her shift started to get something "healthy." The wandering elderly are out in full force getting their shopping done before the big rush after the PTA moms drop their kids off at school, so it's just me and a bunch of bitter old people and it's so early. Why am I not in bed? Why do I even bother working? Maybe I should work at the grocery store. Of course, then I'd probably walk more and go through shoelaces faster.

As you can see, this isn't exactly publish-ready. It doesn't just need editing; it needs a whole spa day in order to be fit for public consumption.

However, this little ditty tells me a lot about the setting. It's a great big mega mart grocery store, presumably in a busy area. We know that because the narrator comments that the PTA moms will create a big rush. We also know that it's 7.30am, and that as a result of the time, the narrator is feeling rushed, exhausted, cranky, and indecisive. This shoelace breaking is the final straw for ruining her day before it even began.

Take a look at your own snippet and notes. How does the setting impact your story? How does the time of day and location of your coziness, best meal, or shoelace incident impact how you feel? How does this lead to how you react, both in physical action and emotional response?

Imagine, for example, that instead of my shoelace breaking at the store when I was already in a wretched mood, it broke as I was getting ready to take off my shoes for the day. How would that story be different? There probably wouldn't be as much conflict, and the reader might start skimming the text out of boredom.

Stories thrive on context, and your setting provides readers with the clues they need to really understand the characters and their motivation. At the planning stage, you don't need to know the entire historical profile and minute-by-minute playbook of what's happening. Create the framework for when and where things are happening, and give yourself room to really explore this territory in the coming pages.

Chapter 4 : What Is the Main Point? (Or, "Why Did You Do This in the First Place?")

Last, but certainly not least, the planning stage is the best time to figure out why you're writing this story in the first place. By that, I don't mean why you have decided to go on this magical, sometimes bothersome path of becoming a writer. We covered that in the first book, and I continue to encourage anyone who thinks they might enjoy the process to give it a shot once or twice in their lifetime.

What I mean is, why are you writing this particular story? Why did you put these characters in this place, doing these things?

Before you panic, let me explain a few things. First, there doesn't have to be a deep sociopolitical undercurrent with moral implications to anything you write. You do not have to aim to be on a college reading list. This is not your doctoral thesis. The only person who ever has to read this story right now is you.

In the case of the folks on the airplane, I was motivated to take the big step from "writing exercise" to "let's try to make a story out of this" because I really connected with the character from whose point of view I wrote the exercise. I used to travel for work frequently, and I was always on flights that boarded before the sun rose. It felt like everyone's crankiness was tuned up to a particularly infuriating frequency, and my automatic response to this plethora of negative over-stimulation was to retreat into a daydream world.

In my daydreams, I would think about how I would react if the most improbable possible person was seated next to me on the flight. Sometimes I'd make the surprise guest a high school teacher, and I would spend the whole flight bragging about how I didn't end up being a loser. A man in a unicorn onesie. Cher in a Bob Mackie gown. Depending on how delirious I was from lack of sleep and anxiety, the person in the next seat would be very real or humorously imaginary.

Therefore, as I started typing out this little writing exercise, I started pouring more and more of myself into this character. And then I decided, why not have the unexpected guest show up? Let's see what would happen from all of those inane daydreams you had circa 2008! Why was I doing this? Because I had started something I hadn't finished, and I wanted to see how it would turn out.

The motivation behind choosing to write this story, at this time, can be something deep and personal. Perhaps you want to demonstrate that a character described as ___ can do ___. Maybe you've been ruminating on a funny voice or character, and you want to see what they can do once you let them roam around on paper a bit. You could have a specific scenario in mind that you'd like to play out, like I did.

Or, maybe, you woke up from a dream and it was such a cool story that you needed to write it out to share with the world.

You don't need to know the end to start writing a story. You may not even know characters' names and demographics. But as long as you have an idea of what your story is about, who does what, and you establish a setting that ties these bits together, you have already started the planning stage. Add in a good reason to write it all down, and you've got the literary equivalent of *mise en place* to start building upon those ingredients and commit to paper the best story you've ever written.

So, how do you know when you're ready to move on from the planning stage? Honestly, you should ride the wave of whatever momentum you have as it occurs. Some of your brainstorming results may be more complete than others. You might find that you have a very clear idea of who your characters are, but that you aren't quite sure how you're going to get to the point where the evil overlord meets his doom. You might know exactly where your yellow brick road leads, but you may not know who you're going to meet along the way. That doesn't mean you shouldn't start tiptoeing down the path to see where it might lead.

When you're working in the planning stage, you might revisit certain aspects of your character's life or what your story is about several times. You might surprise yourself with what is revealed to you about your own story as you continue plotting. It's okay to be indecisive at this stage. Just as you might not know exactly where you want to put the electrical outlets in a house that hasn't been built yet, it's fine if you're still a little shaky on what will eventually be critical decisions.

I highly encourage you to invite your characters to take part in your writing exercises as you develop your story. Audition them. Recast them. Collaborate with them. If your setting doesn't seem right, try typing out a few lines of dialogue in a completely different time and place. This might sound like you're making more work for yourself, but the only thing holding you back at this point is your imagination and your own unwillingness to accept that you are ready to write a story. Stop overthinking, and start writing. You'll be able to check your work later.

Making It All Come to Life

My parents like to joke about how I used to be a perfection-analyst as a young student. I had notes in the margins of all of my novels. I'd underline certain words and explain why the author used those words and how those words worked so much better than any other word the author could have used. I would jot down a few insights into how a particular sentence was important because when the author says, "It was a dark night," they didn't just mean the skies, but the overall mood. I would study the way words were used, and get myself mildly worked up when I felt an opportunity was missed. I wanted to harness literature so that I could develop a close, internal connection to its very essence.

I'm sure this strange activity was based somewhat in the raging self-righteousness of our teenage years, but also out of a sense of duty to literature. Like any curious student, I wanted to take it all apart, see how it worked, then put it all back together and bring it to life. Then I read *Frankenstein* and realized that I wasn't alone in this seemingly psychotic desire, but that it was already starting to backfire on me. By trying to create the most perfect specimen of fiction, I was instead creating a heinously boring story.

No, seriously. I tried to make everything a character. I tried to tell parts of the story from the point of view of a vase on the dining room table. I tried to make every visual a metaphor. The dry, fall leaves landing on the wet pavement demonstrated how precarious humanity is– things like that. Basically, I was passionately flinging everything I had in my writer's arsenal at the wall in an attempt to make it stick. I'd like to tell you that I destroyed that story in a maelstrom of lightning and hellfire, but to be honest, I just don't know where I put the floppy disk I had saved it on. This was 1998– floppy disks were like currency among college-aged writing students.

What I discovered is that you don't have to try hard in order to bring things to life. You don't need to perform artificial respiration on a character that can be summoned with a kiss on the forehead.

Throughout the following pages, I'll attempt to explain how you get from the bare bones of the planning stage to a full-fledged walking, talking story of your own. I am warning you now that there will be little perfection. You will delete large chunks of text. You will find yourself with a really funny feeling in your stomach, like you swallowed a bunch of Tinker Toys that weren't quite put together right. That sensation is called "self doubt." Don't worry about that one- it sorts itself out on its own, as long as you keep writing.

My first book focused significantly on maintaining your mental health and keeping the writing process flowing, so I don't want to harp too long on those points and lose momentum as we head into the so-called "meat and potatoes" of writing your story. At the same time, I think it's very important to acknowledge that writing can be challenging to your mind, body, and emotions. It's not easy to make something up and commit to it so completely that you manage to convince everyone else that it's real. But that's exactly what you're doing.

How do you write? Personally, I recommend writing just as you would talk. My editors hate this, because when I talk, I use a lot of repetitive terms and bold italics, such as saying something is "very, *very*, **VERY** important." It's really not necessary, and by the time you see it as a reader, it's whittled back down to the appropriate number of "verys," which is generally none. But that's exactly my point– you're not done. Just because you put the words on the page doesn't mean you can't keep playing with them. It's not over until you say it's over, so please, don't be afraid of taking the leap. Just face the blinking cursor, close your eyes, take a deep breath, and type or start moving that pen/pencil/quill until you find out what's on the other side.

In the following chapters, we will review how to make your characters become not just believable, but meaningful to your readers. We will follow the trail of events through your world to discover how the plot isn't just about what happens throughout the pages of your story, but what happened before and how the future will be impacted by the events that have unfolded. Then, we will discourse on dialogue, and why what your characters say and how they say it can reveal a lot about who they are and where this story is going.

Along the way, there will be various exercises to help you practice, as you have been previously warned. Since this is a book and not a more interactive format, I'll share the results of my attempts to demonstrate how I applied certain techniques. All of these exercises are raw and unedited so you can share in my own imperfections. I really want you to avoid getting in your own way at this point, so once we've gotten past the writing part, we'll dive deeper into editing and turning the bare flesh of your tale into the perfect being. Or maybe it'll come out hideous and destroy a village. I'm terrible at predicting these things.

Get your writing implements or devices ready, and let's start our journey by getting to know our characters on a personal level.

Chapter 1 : Creating, Developing, and Bringing Characters to Life Inside and Out

Characters are difficult to figure out because people are difficult to understand. You think you know exactly who they are, and then they come thrashing out of left field with something so completely unexpected that you start to question your reality. Is this a glitch in the matrix, or did the Director of Health and Wellness just tell me that she broke her arm drunkenly dancing topless on the bar at a Jimmy Buffet gig? Didn't my cousin have red hair the last time I saw her? Why didn't my friend of decades tell me sooner that she hates Goldfish crackers? The people we encounter in real life are very, very confusing. If you have ever worked in a customer service role, you might already be rolling your eyes and thinking, "Don't get me started." Jim Morrison said it well when he noted, "People are strange."

As a writer, this is both a blessing and a curse. It's a blessing because you get to ride this wild bolt of inspiration through a world of adjectives, actions, emotions, history, and motivation to create your ideal character. It would be like an interior decorator having access to every single swatch ever produced, all free of charge. But, it's also a curse because at the end of the day, you need to dial things back in order for your reader to care about your characters and what happens to them. You can incorporate their designer wardrobe, but if you spend the entire story describing sweater textures, you'll find yourself with a very niche audience.

Let's start by taking a look at what makes a character, then do a few exercises to help you gain a feeling for how you want to share each character with your readers.

Lesson One : Who Are They?

The question the Caterpillar asks Alice as she wanders lost in Wonderland is very loaded. "Who are YOU?" he demands, over and over again.

Deciding who your characters are is a really big task. When you describe a person, after all, you might throw in some physical descriptions as well as personal attributes, such as how they act or where they came from.

As a writer, you have the control to release and withhold as much information as you feel is relevant. However, readers enjoy characters who are recognizable and relatable. Many want to have a mental picture of your characters so they can feel more connected to the story.

Consider some of the most recognizable characters from literature:

- Harry Potter
- The Cat in the Hat
- Gandalf the Grey
- Scarlett O'Hara
- Hercule Poirot

While it could be argued that these characters are only recognizable because they were included in highly successful and publicized movie franchises, the books in which they were first introduced to the world give us a thorough picture of what they look like. Harry Potter has his signature scar. The Cat in the Hat walks upright and wears a bowtie and giant striped hat. Gandalf, "seemed the least, less tall than the others, and in looks more aged, grey-haired and grey-clad, and leaning on a staff." Scarlett O'Hara is famous for her dark hair, green eyes, and tiny waist, while Hercule Poirot is a small man with beady eyes and an impressive set of moustaches.

We know certain things about these characters because writers show their readers these attributes. All of these physical features help us create a mental picture of the characters, but they share far more than how the character looks.

Harry Potter's scar tells us that even as a very young person, he endured life-altering trauma. Though his scar is the result of tangling with Voldemort as a tiny infant, it provides foreshadowing of both the impact his childhood trauma had on his life as well as the events that occur throughout the series. His scar ties him to Voldemort eternally, just as every point in the plot ties back to Voldemort.
Even something that seems like an unnecessary description can be very telling about who a character is. Agatha Christie's Belgian sleuth

Hercule Poirot is described in each one of his appearances as a shorter man with a sleek, clean hairdo and luxurious, well-kept moustaches. These features not only provide a very clear mental picture of the man, but tell us that he is fastidious, attentive to every aspect of his appearance, and precise. As a result, he's going to be the type of person who notices if there is- quite literally- one hair out of place.

As the saying goes, "Beauty is more than skin deep," and that's true of your characters as well. Every detail you disclose to your reader says something about the character.

Here's a mini-exercise to help you put this concept into practice.

Let's look at what you're wearing right now. Describe it to yourself, and then think about what conclusions you might make from the way you just described yourself. Are you accurate?

For example, I'm currently wearing grey, terry cloth leggings that are too big and have paint stains on the right leg. I'm also wearing an unwrinkled, grey t-shirt adorned with a large cartoon mosquito with the phrase "Bite Me." My hair is in a frizzy bun, and I'm wearing giant headphones and glasses.

What kind of clues can we get about who I am from what I'm wearing? Well, the oversized, stained pants might indicate that I'm not planning on going anywhere or seeing anybody. The t-shirt being crisp likely means that it's not one I wear often, which is another clue that I'm spending the day immersed in solitude. Giant headphones and glasses seal the concept that I am in for the day, preparing to focus on something important. The message on the shirt and the activity are somewhat in conflict because I am obviously very serious about something, but also a fan of a good pun.

It might seem like low-level detective work, sussing out all of these clues from something as simple as a choice of pants or shoes. Sure, I might have only put on this pair of pants because it was on top of my clean laundry, but when you're writing, you get to choose what your characters wear and why. Your character won't spill chili on their white shirt and wear their boyfriend's jacket unless you, the writer, make them do so. There are no accidents in writing– just things you let your subconscious get away with.

But a physical description goes beyond what a character looks like. What about the other senses?

What does your character sound like? Do they glide across the floor with no more noise than a moth's beating wings, or do they storm around accompanied by frenzied tympani booms? We all know what a bull in a china shop looks like, but what does one sound like? If your characters speak, the sound of their voice can provide the reader with extra insight into not only their speech patterns, but what it would be like to have a conversation with that character.

Take a look at this line, from Stephen King's *The Girl Who Loved Tom Gordon:*

> *"I've got mine, Mom!" Trisha chirruped in her oh-boy-water-less-cookware voice.*

First, there's the use of the word "chirruped." Trisha could have "said" or "confirmed" but she made a noise shared by small woodland critters and birds. Without any other context, the reader can tell the character is either extremely enthusiastic, or putting on a sublimely controlled act.

Then King refers to the, "oh-boy-waterless-cookware voice." This voice is clearly an act because no one actually gets excited about waterless cookware. Even without the earlier description of this voice, reading this line tells the reader that Trisha is trying her darndest to be happy in this situation.

In addition to how your character sounds, you can share other unmistakable physical features with your readers. Perhaps your character has a very specific smell. Pleasant or pungent, showing your readers how a character smells can be indicative of their hygiene, occupation, hobbies, or bad habits. An auto mechanic might smell of their shop, while someone who enjoys lifting weights might smell of sweat and metal.

Taste and feel don't always have as much opportunity to participate in the portrait you paint of your characters, but don't discount them as possibilities. Writers will often invite flavor into descriptions of romantic scenes, or in the case of strong odor, such as, "I could taste the Aqua Velva he had marinated in."

I think the physical attributes that are felt are sadly underused. Just consider the opportunities you could unlock by describing the roughness of someone's hands. What about a sturdy handshake, or a jiggling hug? Hugging another character might reveal sharp shoulders or squishy arms.

Want to take your character's description to the next level? Sometimes as writers, we need to take these features a little deeper than face value. Often, what we describe has not just physical implications but provides a socioeconomic depiction of the character as well.

For example, consider Jim Hawkin's description of the old sea captain Billy Bones from Robert Louis Stevenson's *Treasure Island*:

I remember him as if it were yesterday, as he came plodding to the inn door, his sea-chest following behind him in a hand-barrow; a tall, strong, heavy, nut-brown man; his tarry pigtail falling over the shoulders of his soiled blue coat; his hands ragged and scarred, with black, broken nails; and the sabre cut across one cheek, a dirty, livid white.

Jim doesn't use the phrase "dirty down-on-his-luck sailor," but just the same, we understand that this is a man who is used to being outside in all conditions, working hard. From his scarred hands to his broken nails, this is not a man who is used to being pampered.

What you say– or don't say– about your characters speaks volumes. So how do you decide when to keep going with the description and when to engage the readers' imagination a bit more? Let's try a little exercise that demonstrates the concepts of "more is more" and "less is more."

Exercise Alert! Nose, Nostril, Nose Hair : Carving a Detailed Character without Alienating Your Audience

The exact words and method you choose to describe your characters depends a lot on your style and the manner in which you wish to connect to your audience. You can decide to describe your character down to their nose, nostril, or even the nose hair.

What do I mean by that? For many people, the nose is the most prominent feature on the face. Describing someone "down to their nose" means providing a visual picture of them that lists their most apparent attributes. If we zoom in just a bit closer, we're headed towards the nostril. This means the description will be a bit more personal and will reveal a bit more about who they are beyond their physical attributes. And if you put your character under the microscope, you'll be able to check out the flora and fauna that call their nostril hairs home.

For this exercise, I want you to pretend that someone has just walked into the room and startled you. Set a ten minute timer and let the words flow freely as you describe this person in as much detail as you possibly can. Go for the whole nose hair experience. Jam in every possible aspect that comes to mind. This doesn't have to flow, and both grammatical and typographical errors are expected. Ten minutes. Write. Go!

Once that ten minute period is up, it's time to read over your nose hair-level description of this person who just rudely barged in on you while you were learning about writing.

Here's what happened when I tried it.

Nose Hair :

It's hard to say which came through the door first: the stink or the man himself. The words "old garbage" comes to mind, but it's hard to pinpoint Tim's odor as coming from one particular source. There was something viscous about him, and I immediately wanted my office carpet steamed and burned.

His eyes could have been any color, but the predominant hue of his palette was red. Broken blood vessels just under his skin created a lacey veil on his rotund and bloated face, and his eyes looked as though there was just enough structure to them to prevent them from bleeding out of his face completely. If the eyes are the window to the soul, Tim had the spirit of a liquor store. He probably cried vodka and blew rye out of his nose.

Contrasting from the floridity of his face, his hair was colorless. It was hard to tell if he had too much or too little, as the strands made a weed-like appearance in random bursts around his face. It was hard to trace each patch to its origin. Beard? Head? Ear? Each sporadic clump was equally matted and looked like it might smudge your hands if you touched it.

I immediately wanted to dip him in a vat of boiling Lysol.

As you can see, I went for broke with adjectives, metaphors, and any bits of decor I could smash into the keyboard in the ten minute time period.

From this description, you could probably draw a decent representation of Tim. Perhaps your nose stung a little as you considered what he probably smells like. You might have had an adverse reaction to the idea of touching his hair.

This is, without a doubt, a wordy description of a character. Often, the term "wordy" is considered a bad thing. We're taught that more is more and to, "show; not tell," but then this "wordy" term comes out, and we all feel we've been naughty. Being unnecessarily verbose is a bad thing. You don't have to use every single word you know in one book. However, there are times when going overboard can be appropriate, and even helpful.

This description of Tim wouldn't fit in every book. If nothing else was described in such detail, this portrait would be completely out of place. However, in a book with a comedic undertone, or one that's going to rely on intense detail to really grip the reader throughout the book (cheers to Stephen King), this might be necessary. If Tim is a very important character, this level of description would be helpful to really dig into his psyche and establish the realities of this world. If my narrator's office actually burned down, for example, these details could be important.

Grotesque oversharing has its place in literature. Equally important, though, is the ability to pare things down.

For the next step, choose a handful of features that you would consider the most important about this character. This time, try to describe the same features without using quite as many words. Be direct and not quite as thorough.

Here's my version of nostril-level description :
Tim is a drunk. He has the typical red, round drunkard's face with broken blood vessels and pouchiness.

He smells awful. He's the type of guy who drinks, vomits, and urinates in the same clothes day after day. His drunkenness has taken over his ability to take care of himself, so he often passes out and awakens in strange places.

This version of Tim is identical in principle : he's drunk, red, stinky, and irresponsible. But notice how the words are condensed. Instead of being as flowery as possible, each description of Tim is direct and to the point. The style is more matter-of-fact, and the tone is plain. This is the type of description you might expect in a medical or police report.

Think about what type of story might contain this description, and what type of character Tim might be to warrant this level of description. Perhaps Tim is an important, but not exactly prominent character. This type of identification would help the reader immediately gain insight into who Tim is without spending too much time doing so. The shape of Tim's character has been established, thus creating a tidy little container for us to store facts about him as we progress through the story.

But sometimes, less really can be more. What if you want to deliver a real punch to the gut description of a character?

Now it's time to show just the nose. This time, write a one or two sentence description of your character. You might find your brain whirring away on this one for a bit longer. Stuffing all of the important details about a character into a tiny envelope may seem downright cruel. I'm not asking you to love the exercise, but to just try it. Just see what happens.

Here's my "Nose" :
Tim was a red, round sort of man, and his stench preceded him. Clad in filth and regret, it was clear that he was a professional drunk.

In two sentences, I established yet again that Tim is red, stinky, irresponsible, and drunk. I changed the order in which these features appeared, but the concept remains the same.

Do you feel the two sentence version has more or less impact than the nose hair version? Which version do you think would make the most sense in the story you are writing?

None of these are "right" or "wrong." Instead, you might find that they have a better home in one story over another.

I encourage you to try this exercise whenever you're stuck in the process of building a character. Not only does this help you gauge the right level and style of description of each person in your tale, but it can serve to remind you how much flexibility you have when crafting your cast.

Lesson Two : How Are They?

Characters are multi-dimensional. They have a physical presence. They have a past, a present, and a future. They not only have and process thoughts and emotions like real people do; they often act on them as well. They bring something to the story through their actions and intentions.

Sometimes, our characters may not change appearance in any way, but who they are at that moment is far different from who they were when originally described. They may be exhausted, or soul-crushingly sad, or really amped up and shaking with excitement.

As a writer, you have a unique opportunity to occasionally hop inside your characters' heads to see what the character is not saying or doing. With this inside access, you can describe your characters' physical and emotional status directly to your readers without your characters having to do any activity.

There are different ways of communicating your characters' physical and emotional status. Take these examples:

1. Sally suddenly drew to a halt, placing her hands on her knees and breathing in loud, short rasps.
2. Sally tried gamely to keep up with the others– she didn't want them to think she was a wimp, after all– but the burning in her lungs was too much.

Each version tells us that there is a female character who got winded. The first is a physical description from the outside. This is what you would see if Sally ran into the room right now. The second tells the events from Sally's perspective. In this version, we understand that

Sally wants to continue running as well as her motivation for doing so– she doesn't want her companions to think less of her. We also know why she ultimately decided to stop running.

Each version shows the reader something different. In the first version, we don't know why she stopped running or what's going on internally behind her decision. In the second version, we can't see her actions, but we know she's in distress from the description of her lungs.

Try this on your own. Choose a scenario in which a character is experiencing a physical problem, and turn it inside out. Perhaps they just got the sleeve of their sweater caught on a door knob. Maybe they need to stop and tie their shoelace, or they dropped a can at the grocery store and it made a loud noise. The actual identity of the character and the activity don't matter as much as your ability to describe what's happening externally to the character as well as internally.

This is another case where neither version is "better" than another; however, being able to give your audience a "sneak peak" at what's going on inside your character can bring more dimension to who they are, which in turn will help engage and excite the reader.

Another way to allow your audience inside the mind of your character is to allow them to quite literally read their mind.

I particularly enjoy this example from Agatha Christie's *One, Two, Buckle My Shoe:*

> *He was a man who was accustomed to have a good opinion of himself. He was Hercule Poirot, superior in most ways to other men. But in this moment he was unable to feel superior in any way whatever. His morale was down to zero. He was just that ordinary, that craven figure, a man afraid of the dentist's chair.*

This is our first introduction to Monsieur Poirot in this novel, and by reading his thoughts, we know a lot about the setting, his character, his emotional status, and the current action. In fact, this excerpt appears at the beginning of a chapter, establishing a lot of details about what's going on without using a lot of words or an overabundance of detail.

There is little physical description in this depiction. Instead, we gather from the man's thoughts that he is uncomfortable on every possible level. We don't know what he's wearing, or what color his hair is, but as readers, we are immediately drawn into his level of misery by the manner in which the author relayed his thoughts.

Every time you write about your characters, consider how you might best convey their current state. Is this an instance where it's more important to focus on physical details, or would your reader be best served by knowing what's going on with your character emotionally, physically, or mentally?

It might seem a bit awkward to describe a character from the inside out, especially at first. I encourage you to practice this trick to help connect your readers to your characters on a deeper level. Let's try an exercise that takes place entirely in someone's head to practice this technique.

Exercise Alert! See Inside Your Character with the Unexpected Guest

You've technically already met this unexpected guest, but I wanted to share the prompt that inspired it.

The goal of the Unexpected Guest exercise is to learn and share as much about your character as possible without them opening their mouth. The premise is pretty straightforward and leaves a lot of room for different possibilities : your character is doing something that is normal for them, when suddenly they discover an unexpected guest.

As I mentioned in an earlier description of this exercise, the guest can range from completely off the wall to not entirely unexpected. The important part is how your character reacts. Stay completely in their head. Focus on their physical and emotional status as well as their thoughts, rather than their actions or what they say.

Just as with the previous exercise, set your timer for ten minutes and off with ye! When you run out of time, wrap up your current thought, then join me again so we can take a look at our results.

Here's what happened when my character found an unexpected guest on an airplane:

She was counting the steps to her complimentary pre-take-off drink. Something about squeezing inside a tin can with a bunch of unwashed strangers before the sun rose made her feel ill-tempered. And the part where these folks were all on their own agenda, stepping on her feet, stopping abruptly in front of her, yelling, coughing, sneezing, and pretty much just breathing in the same space wasn't improving her mood.

"Ill-tempered" might be too kind. She was feeling downright evil. As in, the next person who looked at her funny or asked her to move might be the victim of her very first public assault.

As she resigned herself to being escorted off a plane by TSA while those unwashed mouthbreathers filmed her, she happened to notice Jason Ergway sitting in seat 3A.

Wait… Jason Ergway? THE Jason Ergway? "How Many Ways Can I Kiss You," cover of TeenBeat, the heart and soul of every Gen X girl's sexual awakening JASON ERGWAY?

Saliva and hot battery acid seemed to accumulate too rapidly in her mouth, and she briefly considered reaching for the air sickness bag in front of her. From planning a felony to vomiting on her teenage crush in just a few tumultuous seconds. "How very on-brand for me," she thought with a wry smile.

Apparently that wry smile was plastered all over her face, because Jason Ergway, THE Jason Ergway, looked up at her and said, "Well hey there, 3B. Nice to meet you, too."

Just as the flooded plains of Africa gave way to massive deserts, so too did all the moisture dissipate from her mouth. Now she couldn't peel her tongue from the back of her teeth, and she was fairly certain that the wry smile was now being replaced by a wild-eyed, hysterical sort of expression.

Getting a "behind the scenes" peek at your character's thought process can do a lot for your story. In this case, we know that the setting is in the first class area of a crowded airplane, very early in the morning. How do we know that? Because the character mentally grumbles about it.

We also know that she's in a terrible mood, to the point where she might become violent. We wouldn't know that if I described her actions, because she's not doing anything– yet. However, the fact that she acknowledges the next steps that would occur if she really did act on her emotions demonstrates that she's really considered the consequences.

And then we meet the unexpected guest, who, in this case, is Jason Ergway. We know that he was a teen idol for Generation X as well as the name of one of his most important pieces of work. We're not sure whether he's a singer or an actor at this point, but we do know that he is still very recognizable as the sexy icon he was in the 1980s and 90s.

Lastly, we learn that our female character is not a bold, self-assured type of person. She battles waves of nausea and can't seem to get her face and body to work with her intentions of playing it cool in front of her teenage crush.

Getting inside the head of your characters can reveal much more about them than you might first expect. Looking at things from this character's perspective allows us to experience her emotions first hand, making the transition from anger and frustration to anxiety and awkwardness something the reader can relate to immediately.

Whether you choose to write your entire story from your character's perspective or not, you can use this exercise to help connect with your characters more. When you find yourself unsure of what your character would do next, or find yourself with a character who's getting flat or predictable, consider jumping inside their head for a ten minute writing exercise. You might find a few surprises, including more direction on what's going to happen next in your story.

****

Lesson Three : Why Are They Here?

In the planning stage of your book, you likely drew up a character map, or wrote a list of all of the people you think you might need in your story. At the time, you probably had very specific plans for each of them. Consider this example of a character map from a popular series of books:

This is Character A, and they are the main protagonist. Character B turns out to be their love interest much later in the tale. Character C is B's mother as well as the mother of A's best friend, Character D. Then you've got Character E, who seems like the antagonist at first, but it turns out that it's actually Character F, although Character G definitely gives A a run for their money when it comes to misery and heartbreak. But it's okay because we find out in a later chapter that G was just doing what Character H, their father, told them to do. Only F is controlling H, so basically, F was ruining A's life by proxy. Which is the whole point, because F and A are lifelong enemies.

At first glance, this might seem like an unholy mess. But if I tell you that Character H is Lucius Malfoy, those who have read through the Harry Potter series can untangle this puzzle.

Having a lot of characters can be difficult because you need to remember who is doing what at every moment, and then put all of these actions together. You might feel you need a Marauder's Map just to keep up with everyone!

As a newer writer, you really want to simplify your experience by writing only as many characters as you truly need. That doesn't mean you can't introduce Ralph, the friendly grocer, when your characters need to interrogate people at the scene of the crime or bring in a friendly teacher to share the lecture that ultimately causes the protagonist to make up his mind about his next step. Secondary and tertiary characters can be absolutely wonderful and necessary for moving the plot along. It's just that not everyone who appears in your story needs a full life story.

As you write, think carefully about why each character is present. What do they contribute to the story? How well do we need to know them?

Think for a moment about the "characters" in your own life. If someone were to read a book that followed you through your typical day, how much would the reader really need to know about certain people in order to fully understand and appreciate the situation?

Let's walk through this example a little further. In the book that's based on your life, there's a scene where you look out your window and see your mail delivery person at your mailbox. You're expecting an important check in the mail, so you rush out to see if it's been delivered. As you put on your shoes, your spouse yells down at you from upstairs that the water pressure is low. Distracted, you trip over the cat, and in an attempt to regain your balance, practically tap dance out the front door. Your mail delivery person only sees you as you jig out onto your front porch.

In this scene, who are the most important characters? Who do we need to know the most about?

The "you" character is primary to this scene, as that's the person who is performing the most action. The spouse is also important, because they cause distraction, but not nearly as significant as the cat and the delivery person because they're directly impacted by the clumsiness of the central figure of the story.

Therefore, if you were telling this story just like this, you might go into detail about what your character is doing when they see the mail truck pull up. You might establish that the cat is terrified of the mail truck and runs about maniacally. You could also paint a portrait of the mail person as very staunch, dry, and always serious. However, you don't need to mention that the spouse is using body wash that smells like green apples, or that the cat only likes salmon-flavored treats, or that the mail delivery person has been a devoted vegan… unless any of these facts have bearing on how events unfold later in the story.

For the most part, tiny details such as these are rarely important outside of mystery stories. That doesn't mean you can't write them– by all means, if you find yourself riding a wave in which you are penning the most eloquent description of a bologna sandwich anyone has ever read, keep going. Write whatever comes out. It might not be right for this particular story, but it can find its place elsewhere in your future volumes!

However, you may find that the level of detail you write for each character depends greatly on whose perspective is used for the scene.

Somewhere in the beginning of your story, preferably within the first two paragraphs, you'll need to make a very important decision : who is telling this story? There are several options:

Perspective	Examples
First Person	I woke up feeling refreshed… We followed the train tracks out of town…
Second Person	You woke up feeling refreshed… You and your friends followed the train tracks out of town…
Third Person	She woke up feeling refreshed… They followed the train tracks out of town…

Within the third person point of view, you can choose to let the nameless narrator have full access to all of the characters' actions, thoughts, and emotions, known as "third person omniscient," or you can choose a "third person limited" perspective, in which the narrator only has access to one person's actions, thoughts, and emotions at a time.

To demonstrate the third person limited perspective, compare J.K.Rowling's *Harry Potter* books with the *Game of Thrones* series by George R.R. Martin. While they each have an impressive cast of characters, *Harry Potter*'s narrator is pretty much glued to our Gryffindor hero. On the other hand, the central characters of the *Game of Thrones* ensemble cast each have a turn to tell their story, though only one perspective is used at a time.

Can you use more than one perspective at a time? Technically yes, but it's one of those experimental things that innovative writers such as William Faulkner have attempted. To get a feel for how this works, read *The Sound and the Fury.*

Let's flip back to the scenario with the mail delivery and the cat to practice this concept. When we originally considered the cast of characters, you were the main character, but we didn't really discuss perspective. What is your knee-jerk, first response when I ask you, "Through whose point of view would you have told this story?" :

a) First person: I was staring out the kitchen window when I noticed the mail delivery person pull up to my mailbox.

b) Second person: You were staring out the kitchen window when you noticed the mail delivery person pull up to your mailbox.

c) Third person: (Your name) was staring out the window when he/she/they noticed the mail delivery person pull up to the mailbox.

Now, let's shake things up a bit. What if we made one of the other people present in the scene the main point of view character? Instead of your day as being told through your point of view, what if this scene were told by the mail delivery person? What if the cat told the story or the spouse upstairs?

This brings us to our next exercise, in which we'll put together everything we've learned about characters for one super-fun writing experience!

Exercise Alert! Wheel of Perspective (Super-Fun)

I have great news : this exercise will not be timed.
I have information you might not enjoy as much : it's not timed because you're going to be doing several exercises.

In this exercise, you're going to write a scene from the point of view of each character in it. In order to make this fun, you need to have a scene with at least three characters in it. You can use the "day in the life" example we've been using throughout this discussion, if you like.

Come up with a scenario in which three or more people are interacting on different levels. Then, take a few minutes to write your scene. If you'd like to set a timer for ten minutes here to give you a little structure, that's fine.

Once you've written your scene, read it over, and then choose another character to step into the perspective seat. Rewrite the scene from their point of view. Repeat until you run out of characters.

As you're doing this, experiment with not just the point of view character, but the perspective. Stick to one perspective at a time for the purpose of this exercise.

Here's what I came up with, using the mail carrier/cat scenario:

Version 1:

Every morning, I pour myself a cup of coffee and stand over the kitchen sink, blowing on the hot liquid and appearing to stare out the window. Normally I'm not awake enough to really process what's going on out there, but today I happened to notice Stan, the mail carrier, pull up in his truck.

"Honey!" I yelled up the stairs. "I think your escrow check is here!" As soon as the words were out of my mouth, I realized there was no way she could hear me– the shower was running.

I carefully sat my brimming coffee cup on the countertop and shuffled to the door, exchanging my house slippers for the flip-flops by the door.

"Ed? Can you hear me?" my wife yelled from upstairs. "Ed, the water pressure is shot! Can you do the thing in the basement?"

"Honey, it'll have to wait," I bellowed back, excitedly. "Your check just arrived!"

I'm pretty sure she started to complain, but I didn't really hear much. My mind wasn't processing– I just wanted to get out there and snag that check. We'd been waiting for months, and we could really use the money. I don't want to say things are tight, but they could certainly be more comfortable.

As luck would have it, that's when our cat, Marbles, decided to lose his mind. He does that a lot, hence the name. He came streaking across the foyer, the rug stringing out behind him like a ribbon.

I jumped to the left, shimmied to the right, levitated straight upwards, and prevented myself from falling on my face by grabbing the doorknob. I shuffled on the porch and gleefully performed a high kick just inches from Stan's face.

He didn't blink.

As you can see, I chose to go with the first person perspective in this version. I decided to go with the point of view of the character who trips over the cat, and I named him Ed.

Now, to gather everything we've reviewed in this chapter about characters, let's take a look at what we know about the characters.

Ed: Here's a guy who likes a routine. He likes his coffee hot, but not too hot, and he sets it down gently so he doesn't spill it, which tells us that he's a tidy guy who adheres to his own preferences. He's impulsive and has something of a one-track mind.

Marbles: We don't know as much about Marbles, except that he's a cat, and he's prone to fits of whimsy.

Spouse: She's taking a shower. She prefers her showers blasting, and is perfectly willing to ask for assistance as needed.

Stan: He carries mail and is not easily surprised.

We know that there's a foyer with a rug, which would be familiar in a middle-class home, but we don't know enough to really know that for sure. Thanks to a little jumping inside Ed's head, we do know that this family has been concerned with their financial state, which explains why Ed doesn't want this check to languish in the mailbox.

Now, let's turn the kaleidoscope and take a different view with Version 2:

He was probably downstairs drinking coffee over the sink like he always does, she mused as she fiddled with the water temperature. He's probably going to stand there until the last possible minute, then make some lousy comment about his coffee being too hot, because he doesn't have the patience for it to cool down.

"I'm not going to give in," she resolved to her reflection in the steamed-up mirror. "He can complain all he wants, but I'm not going to say a word."

Every morning Ed made coffee. Every morning Ed hated it. Every morning, Wanda went into work in a terrible mood because Ed had managed to start a fight with her over the coffee he hated.

Not today.

Wanda stood under the hot water and let it rinse some of her grumpiness down the drain. If only Ed knew what an absolute loser he was.

She heard his voice downstairs, raised and excited, but she couldn't make out the words, so she ignored him. Karma immediately struck as the water sputtered, spat, and then drizzled from the shower head. She nodded, understanding her punishment, and wrapped a towel around herself before heading to the top of the stairs.

"Ed? Can you hear me?" she yelled hopefully. "Ed, the water pressure is shot! Can you do the thing in the basement?"

His stupid voice said something that was probably useless. She heard the scrambling sound of Marbles the cat losing his mind, and then a strange, staccato beat on the floor of the foyer. There was a loud thump, then a sound like the door opening. Then silence.

She wondered hopefully if Ed had broken his neck. If Stan– the zombie who brought their mail every morning– found the body, there's no way she'd be suspected of murder. She really hoped Stan was on time today.

This version tells the same story in an entirely different way. From the wife's perspective, we gain a totally new understanding of who Ed is. He doesn't just have a one-track mind– he's obsessed, and he's grumpy when he doesn't get his way.

What's most interesting about this shift in perspective is how our view of Ed changes. In the first version, he was a bit flat. His first person examination of himself didn't reveal any flaws unless he chose to reveal them, while looking at the situation from Wanda's thoughts and emotions demonstrates a totally different man.

As you are writing, you might consider adjusting perspective to provide greater insight into who a character really is. While a third person omniscient perspective provides the most access, you will want to be clear to your audience when you're popping in and out of different characters' heads. Again, *The Sound and the Fury* comes to mind, but let's save the experimental stuff for your second story.

Now let's take one final look at this scene from one last point of view:

After 32 years on the job, you lose the ability to care much. You've seen it all, you've heard it all; and you just want to go home.

Your first stop of the morning is the Elwood subdivision. It used to be nice, and many people still pretend it's nice. It's just got all the tell-tale signs of being a big deal in the 1990s, and few of the houses have changed since then. Maybe someday that's what the kids will call "retro" and everyone will be into it. Heck, what you grew up with as a kid is getting top dollar on those antique television shows.

You normally start at the back of the subdivision and meander back towards the front, but there's a giant package for the Ricardos, and you'd rather have your coffee and a few doughnuts under your belt before you try dragging that thing to their porch. Maybe you'll beat the school bus and those little devil children can help you. They aren't half bad, after all.

So you start at the Evans'. Ed Evans is a real pain in the sack, but 80% of the folks on your route are. After 32 years, you're kind of numb to the average pain in the sack, anyway. It's all part of the job, even though all you do is carry what's been sorted to the mailbox and drive away. Maybe nod or wave if someone is outside.

Normally you'd put everything in the mailbox at the end of the driveway, but of course, Wanda got something in a giant official manila envelope that warns you "DO NOT BEND." You sigh, park the truck with the flashers on, and start the twenty foot trek up the Evans' gently sloping driveway.

As you reach the doorway and raise your hand to knock, you hear commotion inside. There is a thump, and then the door comes swinging open in a single burst. Without comment, Ed Evans high kicks directly in your face, sliding on his other foot.

You can't help but think, "It's too bad he didn't break his fool neck."

And finally we get to see Stan's take on the matter.

What makes Stan's take different from Wanda's take? First, it comes from an outsider– someone who isn't in the household and doesn't have a personal relationship with Ed or Wanda. In theory, we would expect this to be a more objective observation, since Stan isn't intimately connected to these characters as far as we know. As a writer, you may decide Stan and Wanda are having an affair, or that Ed and Stan's father are mortal enemies. The options are infinite.

How did you feel about being in Stan's head in the second-person perspective? Did you picture yourself going through the actions mentioned? Did you feel a different sort of connection or sympathy for Stan than you had in either of the other examples?

These examples demonstrate how changing the perspective changes the reading experience. You've probably heard the phrase, "There's your version, his version, and the truth." As a writer, every version is your version, and they're all the truth, as long as you say they are. That doesn't mean your characters can't lie or misrepresent themselves– it means that you have the ability to decide all sides of the story you are telling.

Putting It Together

So, how does anyone remember all of these things at once? Practice! I wouldn't have you doing writing exercises if they weren't helpful, and each of these exercises allows you to try out different skills and techniques for yourself.

You might find that certain aspects of building a character come to you naturally. For example, you easily hop into a character's head to describe their thoughts and emotions, but you have a hard time actually picturing them. Don't dwell on it. Keep writing. Alternately, you might find that you could identify your characters in a police lineup, but you don't really understand how their moods work. Don't obsess about it. Keep writing.

While your story itself may be on a chronological timeline, the process through which you write the story doesn't have to be. That's why we spent time in the planning stage making notes and writing down all the details that came to mind.

There's this strange state of mind that many writers live in when they write. They just start putting words on the page, and they don't stop. They don't pay attention to what they write, nor do they consciously think about it. It's a sort of internal automatic writing, and thinking about it too much kind of creeps me out.

That's because I, myself, am guilty of this fugue state. I tune out anything in my mind that could come raging in with self-doubt, and I just get the words on the page. Then, once I've reached my stopping point for the day– and I can often feel my quarter start to run out pages before I finally stop– I go back and read over what I've written. Not to see if it's any good, but to make sure my characters did things that they should do and to make any adjustments to my notes. In fact, I usually make a detailed note such as, "Sharon is no longer a cat. I turned her into a kindly grandmother on page 93."

Keep track of yourself as you write, but don't overthink it. Overthinking truly is the creative mind's worst enemy. If you feel that I just introduced a whole bunch of rules that you can't possibly keep track of, consider them more "thoughts and guidelines." Don't get hung up on the technicalities. Just write.

Once you've reached a good stopping point, you can go back and see how you've used the techniques discussed to bring your characters to life. You can play with other tactics and change things up a little to see how it impacts your story. But don't start a giant bonfire or throw your computer into the road. Not now. We do that at the editing part, and we still have a few chapters before we get there.

Next, we're going to take a look at the fun and fascinating concept of dialogue. Now that you have your characters in place, it's time to look at how they communicate with each other, and what that means for your story. While dialogue isn't required in any story, I want to be sure you have all the tools you need to allow your characters to converse and interact as necessary to make your story successful. Therefore, let's take a stroll through dialogue to examine the ins and outs of establishing great communication... between people who don't exist.

Chapter 2 : Dialogue

"In this chapter, we're going to examine the ins and outs of writing fantastic dialogue," she said.

"Oh, really?" he asked.

"Yes," she replied. "I think it's a good idea for new writers to feel comfortable and empowered when writing conversations in their stories."

"If you say so," he replied.

As far as dialogue goes, this isn't a bad example. We know who is speaking and the general gist of their conversation.

But it's not exactly thrilling, nor do we really get a sense of how each person feels about the subject they're discussing.

Let's take a look at the same conversation, only a more dynamic version.

"In this chapter, we're going to examine the ins and outs of writing fantastic dialogue," she explained to her partner across the breakfast table.

"Oh, really?" he asked without much interest. He didn't bother to look up from his laptop screen.

"Yes," she replied with an extra punch of confidence. "I think it's a good idea for new writers to feel comfortable and empowered when writing conversations in their stories."

"If you say so," he replied dryly.

Same conversation. Same characters. Totally different appreciation for what's actually going on in the scene. By adding a few words, this has gone from two people speaking to dynamic dialogue.

There are quite a few different techniques that can be used to spice up your characters' dialogue to make it not only more interesting, but more of an immersive experience for your readers. When used in this way, dialogue can really help move along the plot, share interesting facts about your characters, and help your readers get lost in the world you are creating.

In this chapter, we'll look at how paying close attention to what your characters say– and don't say– as well as the way they say it can help your writing go from words on a page to an immersive literary experience.

Lesson One : To Speak, or Not To Speak

A story doesn't necessarily require dialogue to survive. If you have only one character who doesn't interact with anyone else throughout the course of your story, dialogue would be completely irrelevant to your tale. You are empowered to tell an entire story without anyone speaking.

However, if you choose to do so, think about how you'll define your character. How will you show the way in which they interact with the world around them? What kind of actions will they perform that demonstrate their personality, emotions, thoughts, motivation, and experience? Will you spend the entire story inside their head? For the purpose of a written story, some might argue that even an inner monologue is technically a conversation.

Writing a story without dialogue would be difficult, though many have attempted and succeeded at such a feat. That being said, knowing how to craft dynamic dialogue as well as being able to identify when and how a conversation can really take the story to the next level are very good tools for every writer to have in their literary toolbox.

When characters interact, the reader learns a lot more about each of the characters speaking. In the example I used to start this chapter, we learned that one character is writing a chapter about dialogue, which she's discussing with her partner over breakfast. Her partner, unfortunately, isn't as excited about the concept as she is. In fact, from descriptive terms used in the more dynamic example, we aren't even sure that he listened to what she said at all.

If this example were a story, I could have saved myself some time and typing effort by simply writing the scene like this:

As they chatted over breakfast, she revealed that she was working on a chapter about dialogue. He didn't really pay much attention, but instead continued to read the news from his own laptop screen.

Sometimes this type of summary is ideal for a particular scene, while in other cases, the dialogue version might be far more impactful. So, how do you decide which option to go with for your fiction piece?

First, consider the context. If you've just written a long, intimate bit of dialogue between two characters, you might want to break up the "wall of talk" with a brief summary of what was said next. You want to be sure that the right pieces of the conversation stand out to the reader, so they can focus on all of the delightful details that you included in that conversation. If something like two characters talking about a chapter over breakfast isn't central to the plot or a key point to their interaction, summarizing it allows you to acknowledge that it happened without stalling the action any further.

However, if you've just had a wall of descriptive text, throwing some dialogue into the mix will help break it up, and can even add extra impact to the situation. If your characters have just completed a lot of activity, or something significant has happened, allowing them to have a conversation can reveal a lot about how they're doing physically and emotionally after the action.

One great example of this is the majority of *Harry Potter and the Deathly Hallows.* A significant portion of this text follows Harry, Hermionie, and Ron as they wander around the countryside, searching for horcruxes and avoiding Voldemort. If it weren't for the use of dynamic dialogue in all the right places, readers might not enjoy the journey quite as much as they do.

Furthermore, it's through the dialogue that we find out what the other characters are feeling and what type of impact their travels have had on everyone. Since the books are told from a third person limited per-spective, in which we focus on Harry's thoughts and feelings, hearing from Hermione and Ron directly gives us a glimpse into what's going on in their hearts and minds.

Therefore, as you write your story, consider when and how often your characters should speak. If it's been a few pages since they've spoken to each other, take the opportunity to let them share their thoughts with each other. On the other hand, if having your characters avoid or withhold information from each other helps build the tension in the story and is important to the plot, you might not want them to communicate too much.

Let's look at the dialogue from the beginning of the chapter again. In the dynamic version, we learned that the male character is more or less ignoring the female character. In turn, the female character is either oblivious or pretending to not notice his attitude. What if we gave it more context, however. Let's see how the scene in which the dialogue occurs makes a difference in its impact:

Example 1:

He tried to look calm as he read and re-read the email. He wasn't sure his poker face was working, but she seemed pretty absorbed in her current project anyway.

"In this chapter, we're going to examine the ins and outs of writing fantastic dialogue," she explained to her partner across the breakfast table.

"Oh, really?" he asked without much interest. He didn't bother to look up from his laptop screen.

"Yes," she replied with an extra punch of confidence. "I think it's a good idea for new writers to feel comfortable and empowered when writing conversations in their stories."

"If you say so," he replied dryly. He could feel the sweat building on his brow, and he realized at some point, he was going to have to tell her what he just discovered. But how do you explain to anyone, much less your spouse of 15 years, that you just found out you have a 19-year-old son?

Example 2:

"In this chapter, we're going to examine the ins and outs of writing fantastic dialogue," she explained to her partner across the breakfast table.

"Oh, really?" he asked without much interest. He didn't bother to look up from his own laptop screen.

"Yes," she replied with an extra punch of confidence. "I think it's a good idea for new writers to feel comfortable and empowered when writing conversations in their stories."

"If you say so," he replied dryly.

It was, in every sense of the word, a very normal breakfast in the Bingham household. She continued sipping tea and getting toast crumbs all over the tablecloth, while he looked at sports scores for teams he only vaguely recognized as his coffee cooled.

Lulled into a false sense of security by their cozy routine, neither Bingham looked up when the spaceship landed in their backyard. In fact, it wasn't until the dog started barking relentlessly that they knew something was amiss.

In both instances, this ordinary, mundane conversation stands in stark contrast to the absolutely extraordinary circumstances that are occurring, but in different ways.

The first example shows us that there's a reason for Mr. Bingham's failure to engage in conversation. He's just received some startling, life-changing information, and he's trying to compose himself while processing this news. Instead of ignoring his spouse, he's actually working on a pretty important situation of his own.

The second version establishes the mood of the scene just before something huge and potentially disruptive happens. In this version, the conversation is used to help the reader understand the level of normalcy that exists before things change completely.

Dynamic dialogue can be crucial to the plot in many ways. As the examples we've discussed demonstrate, allowing your characters to converse can help you:

- Gain insight into other characters' thoughts and emotions

- Summarize and reflect upon their experiences

- Establish the relationship between characters

- Create the mood for the scene

- Keep the plot marching along

With this in mind, it's time to try it out with a little exercise.

Exercise Alert! "I Couldn't Help But Overhear."

The first time I did this exercise, I felt pretty awkward. However, it was my writing mentor's favorite exercise, so we did it over and over again, and eventually, I realized that it was extremely beneficial to my writing.

For this exercise, you will need to listen to and write down a conversation between two people. This doesn't have to be as intrusive as it sounds. You can use dialogue from television or a movie. You can write down the conversation you have with your spouse over breakfast, as I did. While it works best when you have no context or understanding of the conversation, there are many ways you can listen to and write down a conversation between two people without being a creeper or a criminal.

You can jot down as much or as little dialogue as you like to get started, but I recommend at least a few minutes so that each party has plenty to say. We'll be using the results of this exercise for the other exercises in this chapter, so make sure you have enough to experiment with in the next topics.

That's it for this exercise. I simply want you to write down a real conversation. No descriptions or dynamics– just save the script. But then, I want you to read it, and carefully think about it from the standpoint of a reader.

Is the conversation boring? If so, what would make it more interesting? If this conversation appeared in your story, would you write out the full dialogue, or summarize it to spare the reader the monotony?

For my example, I'll share the results from one of my collegiate eaves-dropping sessions. This occurred between my roommates in my dorm room, and they were fully aware of what I was doing and why.

S: *I don't know why he's doing this.*
P: *I know why he's doing this.*
S: *He's such a fuddy duddy.*
P: *You said "fuddy duddy."*
S: *What else would you call him?*

P: No, I just don't think I've heard anyone actually say "fuddy duddy."

S: Well, he is one. He's stupid, and he doesn't know how to use a phone.

P: He's definitely stupid.

S: Exactly.

P: Have you called him?

S: Yeah, I left him a message that we were going to Huffman for dinner and told him I'd be free after 9.

P: He's too stupid to know what that means.

S: He's not that dumb. I don't know. I just want him to stop being this way.

What do you think? Keep it, or summarize it? Some of it is helpful. For example, we know that S is the type of person who uses old-timey vernacular like "fuddy duddy." That establishes character. We also know that S is having difficulty with an unnamed male figure, whom P does not like or approve of. We also know that this conversation takes place around dinner time.

Are these useful facts? It really depends on the type of story, so consider whether your dialogue is useful before you invest the time into making it truly dynamic.

Really take your time with this analysis, and think about who you think the characters might be. What are they talking about? Since you are ignoring all context, you have a blank page upon which you can make this conversation work, and we'll practice that in the next exercise. For now, however, I recommend just considering all of the possibilities for your overheard conversation. Think of a few different scenarios for these characters. Change their moods. What if S was sobbing as she spoke, and P was in a fantastic mood? What if it was the other way around? Don't dwell too long on what you think you know about the conversation– just see how many different directions you can take it because (spoiler alert), we'll be doing that in the very near future.

Now that we've taken a look at the many roles dialogue can play in your story, let's dig deeper into how we can make that dialogue even more meaningful.

Lesson Two : Writing a Voice that No One Can Hear

According to Depeche Mode, "Words are very unnecessary / they can only do harm." While they may "Enjoy the Silence," words are pretty essential to the art of writing. However, as writers, we have the opportunity to decide whether the words our characters speak do harm or provide healing.

Each conversation we have in real life is spiked with cues that tell us not just what the person is saying, but what they're *really* saying. There's a significant difference in how we would process these two versions of the same sentence:

"We need ice," he said helpfully as he unloaded the cooler.

"We need ice," he barked, slamming the cooler on the ground next to the van.

Same words. Same activity. Totally different situations.

When we speak out loud to each other, we use different tones and inflections to convey our intentions. Our body language reveals our comfort or discomfort with the conversation, and many of us "speak with our hands," or use hand gestures for emphasis and demonstration. Our facial expressions change as well. We might roll our eyes in disbelief, or wrinkle our nose in disgust.

Unfortunately, readers do not have visual cues available to them. We, as writers, must provide them with this information in order for them to understand. From accents and dialect to facial expressions to any gestures or postures used by the characters, the reader will use their own understanding of the situation to fill in the blanks unless you as the writer do so for them.

That doesn't mean you need to paint every single detail in order to get a full description. Consider these examples:

"I don't want to go," he groaned in disgust.

"I don-wanna go," he howled indistinctly, throwing his baseball glove into the dirt.

"I don't want to go!" He spun around furiously, darting out the front door.

As a reader, you get the picture of how this fellow is feeling without a lengthy, intimate description. He doesn't want to go, and he's either disapproving, on the verge of a temper tantrum, or just ran away, depending on the example.

Each of these lines demonstrates how your dialogue can both paint a portrait of your character and keep the plot moving along. The "tags"-- or descriptions you use of how your characters speak and what they're doing as they speak– can tell your reader a lot about what's happening without saying, "Here's what's happening."

As you write, try playing around with the tags you use. You don't have to tag every single sentence in order for readers to get the gist of what's going on. In fact, as we'll discover in our accompanying exercise for this lesson, dialogue is another situation in which you may need to fiddle around with your words to find the right balance between too much and too little.

But all this talk about how your characters will speak, and we haven't talked about what they'll say!

The words your character uses, and the way in which they use those words, have power. And as the writer, that power is in your hands. One of my mentors used to ask if a character was more of an "ain't, isn't, or is not" sort of person to demonstrate this phenomenon. As in, would it be more appropriate for my character to say, "The toast ain't done yet," "The toast isn't ready," or "The toast is not fully prepared."

Whether your character is familiar or formal depends on the situation, such as who they are talking to and what type of information they are attempting to communicate. It also says a lot about who they are, including their socioeconomic status and adherence to the social norms of the land in which the story takes place. If one of your characters is a dashing rogue of humble upbringing, they might be able to switch easily between voices in order to get what they want. If a character has a doctorate degree in library sciences, they might have a penchant for proper language.

You can also use dialect to share details about how your characters speak. Two famous examples of dialect in action include the characters of *The Adventures of Tom Sawyer* by Mark Twain and Emily Bronte's *Wuthering Heights.*

The subject of dialect is somewhat controversial since it is very easy to slide from "accurate reporting of pronunciation and accent" to "culturally insensitive mimicry." Many modern authors detour around this potential problem by including just a few lines in dialect or giving a hint as to how a character pronounces certain words, such as, "Her Texan twang was prominent, and the server gave her a very concerned look when she asked for more ice in her tea, thinking instead she was referring to his posterior."

Somewhat related to dialect is your actual word choice. My personal favorite is the carbonated, non-alcoholic drink that has divided the entire world. I grew up calling it "soda" because my family from New England called it that. My family from Ohio called it "pop" while my grandparents from rural Pennsylvania called it "fizz," and my neighbors from the South called it "coke" specifically with a lowercase "c", unless it was from the red-and-white label, in which case it was "Coke-Cola."

These regional differences matter when you're writing dialogue. That's not to say that the incorrect name for a dish will hijack your tale, but that your attention to these types of details can enrich the reader's experience.

I always encourage writers to read as much as possible, but I also want to ask you to listen as much as possible. I'm not saying you need to creep around listening to everyone's conversations, but when you interact with others, whether it's in a fast food drive-thru or a benefit at the opera, actively listen to not just their words, but how they say it. What words do they use? Where do they put the emphasis of their sentence? What are they really saying? When they say the performance is, "marvelous," do they really mean it takes their breath away, or are they being sarcastic?

I certainly don't mean to confuse or overwhelm you with the concepts of dialogue, though I know we just covered a lot of information. As always, try not to obsess about doing it "correctly," and instead, focus on how much opportunity you have when writing dialogue. Play around with it. Sculpt and re-sculpt.

To get a feel for how this process works, it's time for another exercise!

Exercise Alert! Way Too Much and Not Nearly Enough

For this exercise, we're going to re-examine our overheard conversation from before. In the last exercise, I asked you to consider the possibilities for this conversation. In this exercise, you're going to make at least one of those options come to life.

We're going to take the conversation and fill it to the brim with subtext, tags and descriptors. Don't leave anything to the imagination. Then, we're going to take the conversation and make it as dull and lifeless as possible.

The order in which you do these exercises doesn't matter. If you'd like to start with a little minimalism, you are certainly welcome to do so. I personally prefer to start big and edit down, so I'll show my "way too much" version first:

Sally sighed as she closed her laptop. She stared out the window for several quiet moments before she whispered to no one in particular, "I don't know why he's doing this."

Without looking up from her Physics homework, which she had balanced on the edge of her bed, since her desk was still set up as a bar from a party the previous weekend. Polly replied, "I know why he's doing this." The sarcasm dripped from her lips in such voluminous quantities that it would have drenched her textbook.

Sally stood up briskly from her desk. She kicked at the brown leather messenger bag that dangled from the back of her shapeless desk chair. She rolled her eyes at Polly, but the other girl didn't catch the gesture, immersed in her calculations of friction. "He's such a fuddy duddy," she said, louder this time. Her voice was gaining strength and momentum.

Polly chuckled softly, the sound of dry leaves rustling in the cool autumn breeze. "You said 'fuddy duddy.'"

Sally whirled around, eyes flashing with sparks of passion and self-preservation. "What else would you call him?" she admonished heartily. Her feelings were clearly hurt by Polly's reaction to her choice of words.

Polly was only partially admonished, and certainly not apologetic as she casually replied, "No, I just don't think I've heard anyone actually say 'fuddy duddy.'"

Sally pretended to be busy inspecting the knickknacks displayed on the wooden shelf above her college-issue particle board desk. She had a plastic model horse, a six inch tall statue of the Virgin Mary wearing three rosaries, a bottle of vodka, and two coffee mugs, one of which was light blue and had a fading picture of a daisy on it, and the other with the phrase "Not a Morning Person" stamped on the side in bold black font. It was another moment before she spoke, but when she did, she seemed to be back on her steel reserve. "Well he is one," she intoned with a stoney voice. "He's stupid and he doesn't know how to use a phone." She nodded to punctuate her confidence in this statement.

Polly finally looked up from the equations she had been furiously scribbling in her red spiral bound notebook. She had to read the room to make sure Sally would be ok with what she said next. "He's definitely stupid," she emphatically agreed.

Sally made many minute and unnecessary changes to the books and papers on her desk as she mumbled, "Exactly."

Polly waited a few seconds to see if there was anything following that statement, then asked helpfully, "Have you called him?"

"Yeah, I left him a message that we were going to Huffman for dinner and told him I'd be free after 9," Sally said with a brief tell-tale glance at the phone, which sat on the floor next to the television. It was clear that she was hoping that he would call right then so she wouldn't have to complain about him. Talking to Billy, her boyfriend of four months, would make this situation so much more bearable. Last night, he had said that she wanted to spend too much time together. He said it made him feel smothered. However, Sally wasn't sure how to deal with a boyfriend who never called or visited of his own accord. He always had to be beckoned, and she had explained this to him in some not-very-patient terms last night. She was afraid that he was still upset and that he would dump her. While it was still very early in the relationship, she was very hopeful for their future together. Furthermore, she had been

dumped brutally by her first college boyfriend just last year, and being on the receiving end of the breakup would trigger emotions she hadn't fully dealt with since her father walked out on her family when she was 10.

While Sally mused on all of this, Polly closed her textbook and her notebook, tucking her pencil into the spiral that held the college ruled sheets of paper together. She really felt bad for Sally's luck with men, but she also sincerely thought Billy was a waste of time, as did 90% of the people who knew him. Still, she couldn't be too harsh on her friend and roommate of four years, especially when Sally looked like she was about to cry. She chose instead to comment on Billy in her normal, flippant way. "He's too stupid to know what that means," she cracked in a joking tone, hoping that Sally would be distracted from her misty-eyed reverie.

Unfortunately, Sally was stuck in her emotions at the moment, and she wasn't about to budge for one of Polly's smart-aleck observations. "He's not that dumb," she whined, her voice rising in tone and volume. She found herself on the verge of crying or screaming and immediately wrestled all of her inner demons to calm and collect herself. She took a deep breath and spoke deliberately. "I don't know. I just want him to stop being this way," she said in a voice that knew the truth, but wasn't sure how to get to that particular destination.

This isn't terrible, but there is very little left to the imagination. I could have thrown in the color of Polly's bed sheets, or what the Virgin Mary statue was wearing, but I was starting to exhaust myself with all of those teeny-tiny details.

Being able to write at this level of detail is important. Sometimes, readers really need to know these extreme details in order to put themselves in the scene. In this case, however, it might be a bit too much information. Just as a magician doesn't start the show with their most amazing trick and a popular musical act doesn't kick things off with their most popular track, you don't want to tell the reader everything they might be curious about all at once.

Why not? First, because it's a lot of information to digest at once. If your readers are overwhelmed before you even reveal what the story is about, they're not likely to keep reading. Also, you're making your job harder as you continue to write. Unless you really want to write a very detailed account of everything that's happening in a character's life and mind, you'll need to spare a few details to develop later. We'll talk a little more about timing in the section about plot development.

Now, let's look at the exact opposite of this overblown, flowery, dare I say "wordy" version of the conversation. This is the minimalist approach:

Sally said, "I don't know why he's doing this."

"I know why he's doing this," Polly answered.

"He's such a fuddy duddy."

Polly chuckled a little. "You said 'fuddy duddy.'"

"What else would you call him?"

"No, I just don't think I've heard anyone actually say 'fuddy duddy,'" Polly said.

Sally spoke again. "Well he is one. He's stupid and he doesn't know how to use a phone."

"He's definitely stupid." Polly said.

"Exactly."

Then, Polly said, "Have you called him?"

"Yeah, I left him a message that we were going to Huffman for dinner and told him I'd be free after 9," Sally answered.

"He's too stupid to know what that means," Polly commented.

Sally replied, "He's not that dumb. I don't know. I just want him to stop being this way."

This version isn't exactly "bad", but it's not really fun to read. My attention started to wander just reading this because there wasn't enough to focus on.

Being sparse with your description can be a good thing, especially when you want your readers to focus on the conversation and the subtext. But in this case, neither character is saying anything that requires great concentration. In fact, if the overall story has very little to do with Sally and Billy's relationship, you could summarize the conversation: *"Before heading across campus to rustle up something edible at their favorite dining hall, Sally and Polly talked extensively about Billy and his lack of common sense. It was how they bonded, despite their many differences."*

Whenever you write dialogue, go forth boldly, and don't be afraid to come back and edit later. Much of what we did in the planning stage will help you with characters, setting, and plot, but dialogue is like a little extra accessory that, while necessary in most cases, can be changed and adjusted as needed.

Putting It All Together

The idea of "dynamic dialogue" is to make sure your characters are speaking:

- In a way that the reader can relate to
- About things that matter to the context of the story
- Without overwhelming or underwhelming the story

As a writer, you are encouraged to "show not tell". When your characters speak to each other, it can reveal more about who they are and their relationship to the plot than simply telling readers who they're going to meet and what they're going to be doing. Telling a story is a creative process, so it's a good idea to not approach it the same way you would writing a grocery list.

There are so many ins and outs when it comes to how people speak that it would be difficult to fully capture all of the do's and don'ts (or "do nots", depending on your character). I've attempted to share some of the most important things to keep in mind as you start your maiden voyage into writing dynamic dialogue, but it can be very overwhelming at first as you stress over how to write the best dialogue.

Don't fear dialogue. It may feel awkward at first, especially as you're getting to know your characters. This is why I encourage spending a significant amount of time in the planning stages to prepare everything before you start writing. Just like two new friends trying to figure out what to talk about, you might find your characters start out speaking in a stilted and awkward manner, but are gabbing like old friends by the time you get to the climax.

Therefore, don't be afraid to write dialogue because you think it might not be "right". Instead, put it all down, and we'll take a look at it again in the editing stage, which is coming up sooner than you might think!

Chapter 3 : Setting the Story with Care

Aspiring writer and professional beagle, Snoopy, from Charles Schultz's *Peanuts* cartoon series, starts each of his stories the same way: "It was a dark and stormy night." That's because he knew, as many writers do, that a story's setting is important for setting the mood and creating the backdrop against which the action takes place.

We discussed crafting a setting pretty thoroughly in the planning stage, so I don't want to spend too much time reiterating what we've already covered. Furthermore, the setting is one of the few instances in which writers can take a deep breath and be objective for once. It's either 1822 or 1701. It's either Kentucky or Pakistan. It's either raining or snowing.

The term "setting" includes when and where the story takes place. And, with a nod to Snoopy, there are what I term "extra special descriptions" that help create the setting as well, including the weather, the season, and other small but significant details that help create a literary backdrop. For example, a character in modern day New York City at 7am in the middle of winter is going to have an entirely different experience than one standing on the plains of Kansas at noon in July 1863.

In the next few lessons, we'll take a look at creating the perfect setting for your story, but don't be alarmed if this goes a bit faster than the chapters on character and dialogue. Consider this your rest period because next comes plot, and it's going to get multi-dimensional again.

However, it's hard to have a plot without a place for things to happen, so we'll start with the setting. Let's shift from portrait to landscape in order to figure out where to put our characters for the duration of your tale.

Lesson One : When Does This Story Take Place?

Time often seems to stand still in fiction, and it can equally hurry along much faster than the pace of real life. If an author has a lot to describe in a single fight scene, it can take multiple chapters to fully flesh out, whereas the actual fight took place in fifteen minutes.

As an author, you have control of the pace, but you need to make sure you don't lose sight of the timeline. If your character was 17 at the beginning of the story, don't make him 71 at the end without helping the reader understand how he aged. At the same time, you can't have a character run a bunch of errands and talk to a lot of people in under an hour– at least, not without some magic or science to help them along.

Many stories hop through time, instead of taking a linear stroll through every day of the characters' lives. Writers have a magic "fast forward" button that allows them to skip over the menial aspects of a day, week, month, or year, and get to the good stuff. You might have noticed how a writer will say, "It was three weeks later when he got the phone call," or "She only had to wait fifteen minutes before she had her answer." These are both examples of the writer using that magic button to keep things marching along.

There is also a "rewind" button. Flashbacks are a fantastic tool for showing your readers an event that occurred in the past, so they can understand why a character is acting or reacting in a certain way. Douglas Adams uses this technique quite a bit in his work to help emphasize the intergalactic setting of his tales. For example, in *The Hitchhiker's Guide to the Galaxy*, Arthur realizes the impact of the end of the world by thinking back to the familiar.

Then he thought of a complete stranger he had been standing behind in the queue at the supermarket two days before and felt a sudden stab– the supermarket was gone, everyone in it was gone. Nelson's Column had gone!

But what about the actual era of the story itself? How do we know where we're fast-forwarding to or rewinding from unless we know when in the history (or future) of the world this book is taking place?

When we read the works of Jane Austen, or Mary Shelley, many of us become a bit jealous at how they have managed to create such an honest depiction of everything from the furniture and rooms inside stately manors to the clothing and hairstyles worn by their characters.

In fact, it was probably quite simple for them, because they were describing what they saw around them regularly. Reading and writing had a different purpose then, and instead of binge-watching *Bridgerton*, people would obsessively read these authors' books. Since their readers couldn't see the pearls dripping down the neck of the wealthy dowager, the authors took to their pens and wrote out exactly what they observed in the world around them. We are very capable of writing what we can see in the "here and now", but we need a little help when it comes to what we call "period pieces", or stories that take place in a historical time period that is not today.

If you were to write a tale that takes place in the 18th or 19th century, you would need to do an extensive amount of research… unless you don't give a fiddle about being historically accurate. If your story leans heavily into fantasy or science fiction, accuracy might be overrated.

At the same time, you can't have characters in 1822 talking about the American Civil War. It hadn't happened yet. You can't have a person drive a Ford Explorer in 1971, because the brand wasn't manufactured until 1990. Things like who the world leaders are, what historical events are taking place, what people are wearing, the music they're listening to, the cars they drive, the food they eat, the way they speak, and even what they do in their spare time rely heavily on the time period in which your story occurs.

.

If your tale takes place in a fictional subculture, such as the undead underground Ann Rice uses as the background for *The Vampire Chronicles*, or takes place in the future, such as with Suzanne Collins' *The Hunger Games* series, you have a little more room for experimentation and imagination. However, even these two examples make actual references to real historical events and follow a parallel timeline to that which has made it into the history books.

Therefore, as a writer, you have a handful of things to keep in mind when determining the "when" of your story's setting:

- Historical accuracy
- The timeline of the world
- The timeline of your character

Deviating from any of these elements isn't criminal, but being mindful of these can help your story stand strong. Readers will be far more in tune and less confused by a story wherein you have a logical path from "then" to "now". And while you can take liberties such as having a character in 1920 eat a sandwich made with Wonder Bread– which was introduced to the public on 21, May 1921– there are some readers who are not afraid to call a writer out on these gaffs.

The most important thing to consider when crafting the time period and timeline of your story is that it remains consistent. If you say something happened ten years ago, make sure your character is ten years younger, both physically and mentally, and make sure the era switches as well.

In fact, that's where our next writing exercise is going to take us.

For this exercise, we're going to create a very specific scene in contemporary terms. Then we're going to change the time period.

For the sake of this exercise, I want you to go to an unfamiliar time. You don't have to nail the historical accuracy for this exercise unless you want practice researching different time periods. Instead, I want you to focus on how the characters may speak, act, and be described differently simply based on the change in time period.

I'll give you a few examples of time periods to get your ideas flowing:

- Early civilization (4000 and 3000 BCE)
- The Renaissance (14th – 17th century)
- The Revolutionary War (April 19, 1775 – September 3, 1783)
- The U.S. Western Expansion ("the Wild West")
- The Summer of 1969

Now I'll give you a few ideas for the scene you're going to write. I've chosen some pretty familiar situations because the goal is to concentrate on how the time period impacts the writing. Choose from the following:

- Two people are gossiping about local events
- Two lovers are breaking up
- A child just stole something that belonged to another child
- A baby is born

You'll want to set your trusty timer for ten minutes yet again, and let the words flow.

First, the contemporary version:

"Well, I suppose it's about time our team did something," Zeke said, nodding his big brimmed hat at the television that hovered above the cashier's head.

Pete wasn't sure anyone was talking to him at first, so he didn't respond. He was still trying to figure out his mileage charts, anyway. Pete didn't like to talk to people when he was trying to figure out important stuff.

Zeke was undeterred. "Y'all follow sports while you're on the road? Do you guys have favorite teams you root for and what-not?"

Pete looked up this time. The only other person in the gas station shop was the cashier, and she was dutifully placing hot dogs on the roller grill for the midnight rush.

"Uh, yeah," Pete said. "Sorry, this paperwork… ," he trailed off, gesturing at his clipboard.

"No problem, man." Zeke said. "Didn't mean to interrupt. Just getting caught up about this playoff game. First time State has made it in twenty years. Kind of a big deal for those boys."

It didn't take much to engage Pete in a conversation about football, paperwork or not, and just like that, he and Zeke were running off stats, savoring the top moments throughout the season, and armchair quarterbacking some of the team's dismal defeats. They waxed poetic about the kicking leg on the sophomore punter and bemoaned that the senior fullback would be abandoning the team with his imminent graduation.

I decided to have my two contemporary characters gossip about the State football team, as that's a pretty normal pastime across the United States.

Now let's see what happens when we put Pete and Zeke in the time machine with the historical version:

"Well, I suppose it's about time our boys got 'round to doin' something or another," Zeke said, nodding his weathered hat at the newspaper. The headline read boldly: 'FRONTIER TEAM TAKES RACE.'

Pete had just pulled into town, and he was tired enough that he wasn't quite sure if he'd hitched his horse correctly. He was so exhausted from the day's ride that he wasn't even sure if he cared. It had been one butte after another bluff all day, so Pete didn't initially respond.

Zeke didn't mind a bit. He was used to strangers like Pete. "Y'all do any racing out there on the range? Or y'all just take your time moseying the dogies from one pasture to another?"

Pete looked up this time. The only other person in the general store was the shopkeeper, and he looked like the type who minded his own business while taking down notes.

"Uh, well, we have some fun," Pete admitted. "Sorry, the heat... ," he trailed off, mopping his brow with a crumpled handkerchief.

"My mistake," Zeke said. "Didn't mean to intrude. I can see you're real tuckered. Just really worked up about what ol' Bill Smith and his horse, Rocket, been doin' out East. They're a hometown pair, and we're all pretty thrilled for the two of them."

It didn't take much to get Pete going on about the topic of horses. After all, he was a ranch man, and horses were his lifeblood. He sized Zeke up to be a horse man, too. Probably rode in on that sleek-looking filly hitched outside, with the broad white blaze on her face.

Before long, they were talking breeding and temperament, and whether a horse could be trained for speed if it wasn't in his blood. It was shop talk, but the kind Pete enjoyed.

In this version, we find Zeke and Pete somewhere in the midst of the Wild West. Instead of discussing football, they're immersed in a conversation about horses and racing. Instead of being at some sort of truck stop with a roller grill, they're at a general store. The television is replaced with a newspaper from the east coast.

How did you do with your version? What details did you include to call out the switch in the time period? What sort of changes did you need to make to your characters' descriptions, dialogue, or the content of their discussion?

You may have found it harder to write the second version. Most of us don't have any insight into historical periods in which we didn't live, so figuring out the details might have been a little trickier.

While not every writer attempts to write outside of their time frame of reference, it's a good idea to practice the idea to help keep your skills fresh. A quick flashback could have historical ramifications, and it's important to be cognizant of timelines in your tale. You never know when you might have to hit fast forward or rewind!

Lesson Two : Where Does This Story Take Place?

You might be wondering how I can possibly have multiple pages of discussion on the "where" aspect of setting. Honestly, I don't. Even if you're writing a story about bilocation or multi-dimensional travel, you still can't actually describe more than one place to your reader simultaneously. Words on a page are here and now, and most people can't read more than one sentence at a time. Therefore, your location doesn't require nearly as much molding and crafting as some of the other aspects of writing.

That doesn't mean you should neglect your location. Readers like to know where they are when things are happening. The location generally includes an immediate space, such as a character's living room, a corner shop, or the school bus, as well as a general place, like Cleveland, Southern California, or the Spanish countryside.

How much you say about a location depends on how much you want your reader to look around and observe it. For example, if your character runs into a grocery store to grab a bottle of water, we don't need to know the store mascot, the arrangement of the aisles, the county in which it is taxed, and the map coordinates of the parking lot... unless those are pertinent to the action. If your character slams into a person dressed as the mascot as they're dashing into the store because they're preoccupied with the dehydrated space alien in their passenger seat, that quite literally changes the story entirely.

Setting the scene is just as important as creating multi-dimensional characters and dynamic dialogue. Imagine if *Gone with the Wind* hadn't taken place in the American South during the Civil War, or if the Connecticut yankee had ended up on Billie Jean King's tennis court. Consider how the characters change and the plot progresses based on where the action takes place. Being in the path of Sherman's March to the Sea was the direct cause of many of the events in Margaret Mitchell's novel, while in *A Connecticut Yankee in King Arthur's Court*, Mark Twain's protagonist is only able to fashion himself into a "magician" and befriend King Arthur by taking advantage of the limited knowledge of the citizens of England in the Middle Ages.

In each of these examples, the location is more than just a place where things happen. Scarlett O'Hara has a pampered and privileged life, and being in a location crucial to the events of the Civil War changes her life in many ways. If Tara was located in Minneapolis, this would be a completely different tale. The life Scarlett knows and loves is disrupted largely because of where she is, and in fact, one could also argue that many of her philosophies and ideals are formed through her rich Southern plantation upbringing.

On the flip side of the coin, Hank Morgan's only familiarity with medieval England is through Sir Thomas Malory's *Le Morte d'Arthur*. In the industrious spirit of many Americans during the Technological Revolution, he sets about changing his world to meet his expectations, instead of adapting to his situation, as the equally intrepid Ms. O'Hara does.

Your setting does not have to be poignant and meaningful. Your setting may only be incidental to the focus of your story.

Remember in the planning stage, when I asked you what your story is about? As a writer, you have a choice as to how much or how little your setting impacts your story. Here are a few questions you can ask yourself when trying to decide how involved you should get in describing your setting:

- Does it matter if the scene takes place in an urban or a rural location?
- How much travel do your characters need to do in order to accomplish the actions you've chosen for the plot?

- Would this scene unfold the same way indoors and outdoors?
- Do you need to have a lot of people present in order for the scene to work?
- What would happen if you moved the scene in space in time?
- Do your characters interact with the setting at all?
- Do you need your readers to recognize and recall this location?
- Will your characters return to this location?
- Do your characters have an emotional attachment or need for this location?

As you may have gathered by now, writing is a very "soft" science. That is to say, as long as you are proud of the outcome and feel that you have imparted to your audience everything they need to know in order to follow the story successfully, you have completed the task to satisfaction. A bland story can be very successful. A super flowery story can be just as enjoyable. Different readers love different writing styles, and as someone who has done extensive editing and critiquing in the past, I would never assume to tell someone they have written something "wrong".

Instead, consider how questions such as these impact your story. Your readers will no doubt have questions. It is your job to determine how many of those you want to answer directly, and how many clues you want to hide in other areas of the book. Your character descriptions, dialogue, and setting all help the story go from "good" to "great", but the way you use these in-depth "showing" experiences isn't dependent on some very specific if/then rules set in stone by the literary greats. It's all in the way you put things together.

Before we head too far off track being poetic about prose, let's head back to the setting, specifically. We've chatted quite a bit about characters and dialogue, after all!

Many authors do a fantastic job of revealing the setting to their readers, and providing just enough detail to help the audience connect and understand what's going on. But one important consideration is who is describing the surroundings. We've discussed what the setting means to your characters, but how do they actually interact with it?

To learn a little more about how perspective and setting intertwine, let's try an exercise that requires us to do just that– consider the setting from multiple points of view.

Exercise Alert! The Familiar and the Unfamiliar

Any time you start to dive into a world of description, make sure you tilt the lens so that you're looking at whatever you're detailing as someone in the story itself.

This exercise will help you appreciate the relationship between character, perspective, and location. You can even throw some dialogue in, if you'd like to practice that as well.

Your goal is to describe the same location from two points of view. The first will be from the perspective of someone who is very familiar with the location. Just as Scarlet O'Hara had a deep and intimate knowledge of Tara, this first description of your location will be from someone who has spent a significant amount of time in this place.

The second description will be from someone who has never visited or even considered appearing in this location. Much as Hank Morgan unexpectedly gets zapped to King Arthur's England with no forewarning, let's pretend this character genuinely has no idea where they are. Try to pick a character who would be super out of place in this setting- the more bizarre, the better.

To make things easier for you at first, I ask that you describe your own home. Whether you live in a house, cabin, or van, think about how someone who is very familiar with your home would describe it. While you are welcome to do this from the first person perspective, you can also take the point of view of a friend, relative, or pet.

Set a timer for ten minutes, and show us your home.

Here's what I came up with:

When I walk in the door, the first thing I see is the floor. I hate the floor. Someone got the brilliant idea to tile it, and they didn't do a very good job. The tile is a weird orange color that has nothing to do with the rest of the house. I don't think anyone bothered to level the base first, so it has a similar topography to the hillside into which our house is built.

Then there's the grout. Its black stains have so far been resistant to three different professional "solutions" which means it's probably extraterrestrial, and I should be afraid. Instead, I'm more irritated by the orange and black spotted terrain that exists just inside my beautiful hand-carved front door.

The worst part is that there are four very spacious, accommodating closets in my entryway, which means I'm constantly hiking the hills and valleys of that tile. Thankfully, we had the foresight not to put anything fragile in those closets, because in the seven years we've lived here, no one has passed through without stumbling a little on the uneven surface.

It takes a certain level of familiarity with a location to be this obsessed with how much you hate it. Most people don't walk into a place for the first time and immediately gasp over how wonky the tile is. To demonstrate, let's take a look at how someone who is unfamiliar with the location would describe this entryway.

I don't understand. I can see inside, but I can't walk inside. There's a big noise, and things move, and suddenly, I can walk right in.

But I don't want to. The ground feels weird. It's flat and cold. There's nothing to eat on it. My feet are uncomfortable. and I can't find anything to grip. Some parts are smooth and shiny. I don't like those at all. The other parts are kind of rough. Those feel a lot better to my feet.

Everything is so tall. I'm used to everything I need being right in my line of sight, but here I have to look up to find anything. I can't even find my way out of this place. It just keeps going. The texture beneath my feet changes, but there's no grass or dirt. It's so slippery.

This time, I chose to write about my entryway from the perspective of a chicken. It's not obvious because I spent all ten minutes trying to think like a chicken!

I don't actually like this version. I think it's boring and repetitive, and not at all interesting. I cannot impart upon you enough how important it is to let yourself write things that you don't like. By catching yourself doing something you think is terrible, you understand a lot more about your strengths and weaknesses as a writer. From there, you can work on those areas where you aren't up to your own standards.

You can practice the things that make you twitch in fear. You have control not only of your characters' destinies, but your own as well.

And, speaking of destiny, it's about time we got on to the part where we talk about plot.

Putting It Together

The setting of a story is a key detail that your readers likely need to know in order to get the full picture and become immersed in your story.

The time period in which your story occurs can impact who your characters are as well as what they do and why they do it. The words they use and the manner in which they speak can also be influenced by when they are living.

The physical setting can also be much more meaningful than "the place where the things happen". Your character may interact with and be influenced by the setting. Their understanding of the world around them dictates their behavior which makes it very helpful for the reader to know what the world around them is actually like.

When you're writing details about your setting, I recommend erring on the side of too much. I also encourage you to fiddle around with the details to make sure the time and place is exactly right. You don't need the accuracy of H.G. Well's *Time Traveler* to get there, but you do want to be certain that you have written your story in exactly the right time period for each event in your tale, whether present, future, or flashback.

Writers are often tempted to describe the setting through their own eyes, but I encourage you to pause and re-examine your character's surroundings from their own perspective. Is it familiar? Is it strange? What do they think of it? What is confusing?

The setting doesn't need to be described down to the glaze bubble on the rim of a vase that appears on the mantle top, but the beauty of the literary arts is that it can be. In fact, you could write an entire story from the perspective of that glaze bubble, if you wanted to. I encourage you to be consistent but also curious about your setting as you show your readers around this amazing world you have created.

Chapter 4 : Planning Your Plot, from Then to Now and Tomorrow

There are likely a few of you who have been reading this book with a certain level of anxiety that I've only made a few references to the plot thus far.

It's really a "chicken or the egg" kind of argument. Many writers prefer to develop the plot first and get the entire timeline dot-to-dot connected and solidly in place before they start sketching in the details of characters, dialogue, and setting. Others insist that if you do a bang up job with those elements, the plot more or less just moves itself along organically.

I say : Why not both?

Going back to our house analogy at the beginning of this book, it's true that you need to lay the footprint of a house before you build it. This is why I encouraged you to be very detailed not only in "what's it about" but "what's the point" in the planning stage. The reader doesn't know any better if the protagonist and antagonist were supposed to meet for a laser gun showdown in Muncie, Indiana or a car race down the Las Vegas Strip as the final climactic event. They only know what you put on the page.

Therefore, my thought is that you should have the groundwork, skeleton, frame, or whatever you need to start building, but the process that you follow after that is a matter of doing what you need to do to make your vision come to life.

Someday, you will have a technique. Just as someday, you will be able to sit down and bang out a cute little short story (or famous gothic horror novel!) for your friends and family as a sweet party trick because you find it so simple to organize your thoughts with your tried-and-true method. But as a brand new writer, I don't find it helpful to focus on meeting the demands of a highly structured technique. I have participated in forums in which those who were trying fiction writing for the first time would be absolutely decimated by critics who would get hung up on grammar and technicalities in a first draft.

Personally, I don't think that's fair. A first draft is the best place to make all of your newbie mistakes. And while correcting and providing feedback on grammar and technicalities is certainly useful in the learning process, I feel it's far more important to get the whole story down before you start fixing it when you're attempting to write for the first time. Build the house before you put up the wallpaper.

Why? Simply because it takes a lot of energy and momentum to write a fiction piece from start to finish and feel proud of what you've done. If you're getting hung up on punctuation before you complete your first page, you're going to talk yourself out of continuing your book very quickly.

Furthermore, techniques change. The way I write now is very different from how I was trained to write 30 years ago. In those days, em-dashes and en-dashes were very edgy, and you only used them if you were too artsy or grammatically ignorant to use the preferred parentheses and semicolons. I had to rewrite an entire semester's worth of theatre analysis because I occasionally started sentences with "however". Today, I can get away with those things. I've had to learn how to write again several times in my career simply because the rules are always being rewritten. The technical stuff is subject to change, but the passion and perseverance you put into constructing your story is eternal.

So, when it comes to plot first or not, I would consider myself Team Eyes Up. Pay attention to your plot. Keep your planning notes close to you. As I mentioned earlier, make notes when things change because those alterations will nearly always trickle down to the rest of the story. But don't feel that you have to introduce a new plot point every 2,500 words to be successful. Don't feel that you are forbidden from putting two different conversations on the same page, especially if they help your story get to where it needs to go.

Keep the plot in the forefront, but let your writing explore this world that you are creating. Find out where your creativity wants to go. And, if it turns out that you were right on par with what you planned in the beginning, then you've done a fine job. If you end up writing a completely different book because you realized that you were way off when it came to your protagonist's motivation, you've also done a fine job.

If you're hoping to read this section to get exact details on how to keep your plot marching along without giving too much away, I'm afraid you'll be disappointed. However, if you're looking for some pointers to help you navigate the unfamiliar waters of your very first fiction venture, you've come to the right lighthouse.

Lesson One : How Do We Get from Point to Point?

In a nutshell, the plot of your story is what happens. More descriptively, it's all the things that happen from the first page, through the rising action, to the climax, and throughout the falling action. Every action and activity that your character participates in feeds the plot.

This is probably one of the harder things to keep in mind as a writer, especially when you're getting caught up in the story. You might find yourself adding in extra steps and scenes that don't really need to exist just because you see them unfolding in your mind, and you have the perfect dialogue for that scene. Allow yourself to write it, but also, give yourself permission to take it out of your story if it doesn't add anything to the overall purpose.

The main concepts to keep in mind when constructing a plot are action and reaction. Action is what your character does. For example, *"Tim threw the ball towards Jimmy."* The reaction is how others– or the character performing the action– act as a result of what has been done. *"Jimmy ducked. 'Leave me alone, Tim!' he howled."*

Each action you include in your plot will likely have at least one reaction in order to be important to the plot itself. That reaction can be emotional, physical, obvious, subtle, or even delayed for a long period of time.

William Shakespeare might be considered one of the founding fathers of writing action versus reaction. While he is not a novelist, but a playwright and poet, the man could put together a fantastic plot. The roadmap is delightfully easy to follow in each of his major works: Because Character A did this, Character B did another thing. Then Character C did yet another thing, but Character A thought it was Character D, so A did this other thing to D and started a fight with B.

Pace is how quickly or slowly these things happen. Typically, a fiction story starts slowly, allowing the reader to get invested in the story before the action picks up. Then, as we climb closer and closer up the rising action, the actions and reactions happen more quickly. The climax of the story is an explosion of tension,conflict, and drama. Then, we put everything back together and reveal what has happened as a result of that combustive situation.

Each story has a different pace. The climax of a story does not have to occur on a specific page. Some authors– Stephen King comes to mind again– have a way of carefully creating a sense of normalcy with a slow pace and what initially seems to be hundreds of pages of interesting but pointless actions. Then, for the big scene, everything makes sense, all of these actions come together, and there's often a literal big boom or battle that rearranges reality. Everything the characters did along the way was setting up for this big moment, giving the reader a fully different appreciation of what everyday life means in the long run.

In contrast, you have short stories like O. Henry's *Gift of the Magi*, in which we follow one character's every thought and footstep through the day, have a big reveal, and go eat pork chops. It's quick, and it gets to the point very bluntly.

Whether your characters' reactions are immediate or involve slow-burn revenge, what they do and how they do it depends on who they are as a person. Their reaction will either be exactly as expected, indicating that this is a characteristic response, or it will be completely out of the blue, which demonstrates that something drastic has changed within that character.

This lesson's exercise will help us try out action, reaction, and pacing all at once, with someone acting entirely out of character.

Having a character act the way you expect them to is rewarding. When a character acts, well, uncharacteristically, it makes for a special scene.

In this exercise, we're going to come up with our own hero or heroine, and have them do something totally unexpected. As in, I want you to think about the last thing in the whole wide world you might think this character is capable of. You have my permission to get as weird and wild as you want here. This is one of the few times where using a stereotype to build a character is actually permissible.

However, I don't want you to be in a rush. Much like the tiger stalks the gazelle, I want you to take your time getting to the big moment. The goal is to build the momentum in this exercise much as you would build the rising action in a story. But here's the catch: you only have 15 minutes to do it.

Therefore, you're going to have to figure out what the actions and reactions will be within a very short period of time. I recommend making them all immediate, unless you want to pull out your magical "fast-forward" button to skip a few things.

Here's what I came up with:

As a rule, she never came to this coffee shop. It was always so crowded– so crowded that she could tell she would be uncomfortable just by peering through the steamed windows. So the mere act of being in line, in this particular coffee shop, which she passed each day on her walk to and from the library and her home, was fully out of character.

She was debating whether or not she should accept defeat and leave when a man who could only be described as the most generic stereotype of a businessman began looming in her direction.

It was possible that he had been behind her in line this whole time, but she didn't think so. She felt as though she would have noticed his utter cartoonish manifestation of the white collar archetype. And yet, here he was, breathing angrily in her direction.

"I'm next," he said, stepping in front of her, one agitated wing tip at a time.

What she said came from a place of confusion. She was so shocked that someone had spoken to her that she had failed to listen. "I'm sorry for that," is what came out of Lilly's mouth.

He gave a shudder, like a monument weathering a tremendous earthquake. His voice bellowed with authority and audacity. "I... SAID... I'M... NEXT!" Each word was punctuated with a capitalized pause to emphasize meaning.

"Oh. I thought I was." Lilly was still confused. She'd been concentrating on her own discomfort with such precision, that this silly stranger's inability to understand how queues work seemed meaningless. "I just wanted a tea. My Thermos broke." She held out the leaky vessel with its cracked lid to demonstrate.

With a wild racket, the Thermos became airborne as the businessman smacked it out of her hand. Channeling the ferocity of demons escaping prison for the first time, he howled. It was a long, braying sound, like an exquisitely executed trumpet solo. No words, no notes, no structure, just pure tone and breath.

And that's when Lilly came to herself. Her bookish self, which spent all day enforcing silence and making teenagers spit out gum in an appropriate place, realized where she was, who she was, and what was happening, all in that instant.

"Rot in Hell, A##hole! I just ... want ... a... TEA!" Her voice rose to a full yawp that God and the whole country could hear. The entire coffee shop became silent, and those words, which she had never used before today, reverberated in the stillness.

I decided to have a librarian loudly and publicly curse out a business-man in my version. Libraries are generally pretty quiet places, and the dichotomy of the librarian out-bellowing a self-absorbed, loud customer amuses me.

I also wanted to put the concepts of introvert/extrovert, quiet/loud, nervous/excited, and timid/outgoing to watch them bump against each other. That's why I took my time making the characters act and react to each other, instead of having Lilly reach up and slap him, which was actually my first instinct. While satisfying, I chose the loud direction so I could explore the characteristics I gave my character.

What happened in your version? How many actions/reactions did you manage to create before you got to the big boom? What details did you include to help the reader understand the extremes between how the character is expected to act versus what they actually did?

Exercises like this allow us to explore many different extremes. In fact, I recommend coming back to this exercise any time you aren't sure whether your character should do the unexpected so that you can check out all of the potential "what ifs" and see what would change if your character acted outside of their type.

The plot is made of lots of little and big things, just as our daily lives include equal parts monotony and excitement. Your goal as a writer is to move your reader through those little and big things in a way that is meaningful, insightful, educational, moral, entertaining, and/or informative. Whether that means taking them directly to the point or carefully constructing a world only to bring it crashing down is up to you.

Putting It All Together

Well, that's it! That's how you write fiction!

... Or is it?

How do you feel right now? Are you excited and inspired? Perhaps you feel even more intimidated about the writing process than you did before you started this book. Both answers are correct, as are any other feelings you might have about starting your first fiction piece.

There are some writers who have a very specific formula for starting a story. You might have received homework in school that asked you to very clearly write out the plot points. You might prefer a very structured character map. I encourage you to follow these methods if they help you stay on task and maintain your focus.

However, if you find that you're trying too hard to fit the format and losing track of your muse in the process, I recommend you stop trying so hard. As I mentioned earlier, the technical details are forever changing. Getting through your first fiction piece is a feeling you won't ever forget.

Earlier, I recommended not starting on the writing stage until you feel confident in the planning stage. I hope that our investigation into the attributes of characters, importance of dialogue, requirements of setting, and plot points has helped you appreciate why I issued that warning. My addendum stands, however, that if you simply cannot hold in a snippet or scene that is begging to be written, you should absolutely write it down before you lose inspiration.

Writing books is funny like that. You'll think you know exactly what you're going to say next, only once you type out one word or punctuation mark, you immediately forget what was supposed to follow. Or, even worse, you'll type out a sentence only to re-read it and discover that you've written something almost incomprehensible.

Several times, I have encouraged you to keep the concepts I have introduced in mind without focusing on them too terribly hard, and that's because writing is basically juggling words. And just as those who juggle balls, bowling pins, or chainsaws don't start with dozens of objects in the air, it's much safer as a brand-new writer to allow yourself the opportunity to return to and finesse your work through the editing process.

Making mistakes is part of the process. I can't tell you how many times I've looked at the screen thus far and thought, "What have you done?" I have used "to" instead of "too" simply because I'm rapidly pounding on the keyboard and missed the second "o". I have managed to confound the autocorrect feature when my fingers reflect my excitement. At one point, I used the word "detail" three times in one sentence. I also took time off from the letter "l" and started typing "/." That's a lowercase L and a forward-slash, if your font settings don't display the difference.

Don't expect to be perfect. Don't try to be perfect. Do your story justice. Make your characters come to life. Bring the reader so deep into the story, they don't want to leave. Show the reader the world in which they now dwell, and take them on a voyage they'll never forget. Earlier, you defined why you were doing this; why you were writing this story, that is.

Now go do it. And once you've said everything you need to say, it's time to go on to the part where you make it even better.

Making It Really, Very, Super, Incredibly, Amazingly Good (The Editing Part)

The long-awaited, oft-mentioned editing part of the book is here, and I'm afraid it's not going to solve any of your problems.

That's because editing is less about building a house and more about making it lovely to live in. Some remodeling efforts are quite minimal–such as changing the paint color in a room or adding draperies. Some are extensive. You might choose to add a room to your house or remove a wall. Either way, you know it's a good idea not to make any permanent changes until you've lived in it a bit to see how it feels. Otherwise, you'll end up changing it over and over again in pursuit of perfection.

Writing fiction is very similar. You can only make so many major changes before you've got an entirely different story than that which you originally wrote. Plus, it's extremely easy to explore more and more possibilities, especially when the person who wrote the "How To" book you consulted specifically told you to keep experimenting.

I've repeatedly visited my disdain for new writers getting hung up on process and structure, but allow me to recommend a few mostly unstructured steps for successfully editing a book without driving yourself up the wall:

1. Experiment during the writing process.
2. Submit your first draft to yourself for editing.
3. Wait several days before you start the editing process.
4. Allow yourself time to forget what you wrote.
5. Only change things if you really don't understand why you did that.
6. Otherwise, continue to polish the woodwork, shape the hedges, select or subtract knick knacks, or whatever you're doing to spruce up– but not change!-- your creation.

"Ok, but how?" you are likely wondering. And for that, I have a few tried, tested, and tortured tips for knowing when you've hit a homerun with your fiction piece.

Tip #1 : Don't Count Words; Make Words Count

"Is it a novel, a novelette, or a novella?" she asked.

I couldn't answer, because it hadn't mattered until that exact moment.

Unless you are writing a piece specifically so you may submit it for publication, you don't need to know the answer to this question. You should think about it, but as I've mentioned, you don't need to marry yourself to a format until you feel comfortable writing fiction. Therefore, you do not have a required word count, so stop adding or subtracting for the sake of size.

Most writers find it awkward to read a piece after it's been completed. Some of them ship it off to editors before they reread the first draft because they know they'll be far too hypercritical of what they've done. I admit that I find it hard to relax and really get into the stuff I write, simply because I put so much pressure on myself. I can't tell you how many times I've stared wide-eyed at the screen these past chapters as the sickening feeling that I've done it all wrong sweeps from fingertip to toe.

It's because of this awkwardness that I recommend waiting a bit before editing so that the piece isn't as fresh in your mind. You don't need to have a fight with yourself, and you don't need to get Ernest Hemingway-level drunk to cope with the creative process. Shake it off and come back later.

When you feel your eyes are once again fresh, it's time to read through the whole thing. Read it like a reader, not an editor. Don't look for weird spacing and errant semicolons. Instead, ask yourself three questions:

1. Is it too "fluffy"?
2. Is it too vague?
3. Did I have to work too hard to understand what's happening?

"Fluff", or excessive wordiness, isn't always a bad thing, as we discussed earlier. In fact, there are times when a reader wants you to give them heaps of fluff. However, this is a piece of fiction, not a room full of plush toys, and not everything needs to be fluffy.

As a reader, were there moments in your story where you felt like you were skimming over a description? You wrote the thing, so you know what happens. When you find yourself skimming, it's a tell-tale sign that what you've written isn't entirely necessary.

Should you find yourself in this situation, take out the fluff, and see what happens. Don't trash it– just hold it to the side for a moment, and re-read the passage without the fluff. What changes? Does anything make more sense? Do you still get the same emotional impact and understanding of the story without it? Is it still interesting?

Detail is not a black/white situation, either. It might not be a matter of "keep it or cut it", but a matter of choosing which details are the most important, and what you're trying to convey. Think back to the "Nose, Nostril, Nose Hair" exercise. How much do we need to see?

Similarly, how much is too little? While a story doesn't have to be uplifting or hilarious, it does have to be entertaining, in that it captures and compels the reader. A vague story is still worth reading, but it might not have much of an impact on those who read it. Part of the beauty of the creative process is allowing your imagination to soar, and interpreting the thoughts, feelings, and images that come to mind into art that you can share with others. Writers create art through the use of words, and withholding a description is just as detrimental as holding back on the colors in a landscape.

Furthermore, it's not fair to have the reader work too hard. While subtext is a delightful toy for writers to play with, many readers appreciate it when a writer checks in to make sure they're following along. If everything in your book is a metaphor, throw your reader a few clues so they can make their own decoding key. A good story is like a puzzle, but the writer should provide all of the pieces.

Throughout this book, we've tried a variety of exercises that work with the concepts of less and more. We've visited all sorts of extreme lands, and found our way from one opposite to another. In many cases, you'll find the ideal level of detail is somewhere in between the two, which means the writer has the opportunity to slide up and down through the scales to find the right spot. Enjoy this privilege, but don't abuse it.

Tip # 2 : Keeping It Real

Is your story engaging? Is your story confusing? Does it read like it was written by a committee or one very dedicated person?

Hardly anyone plops down and writes a story in one sitting. Most books and longer pieces of fiction are written over the course of many days, months, or even years. And because writing is so immersive, as with the juggler and the many flaming chainsaws twirling above their head, many writers lose track of themselves in the process.

Therefore, I submit you three reminders as you read over your manuscript for the first time:

1. Tone Matters
2. Tense Matters
3. Perspective Matters

The scenes you write should reflect an emotion appropriate to what's happening. As writers, though, it's very easy to capture our own tone in the way we write. When you're in a great mood and the words are flowing easily, you might come across as chipper and confident. The words you use will be spot on, and your descriptions will be impressive. When you're in a lousy mood, you might find that the words leap off the page with the enthusiasm of a news reporter who is ready to retire.

This is another reason I recommend stepping away from your story for a bit before you edit. You'll likely remember exactly what was going on the day you wrote the various scenes, and if you re-read them too soon after, you'll be able to relate the tone to how you felt on that day. Whereas, if you read after you've given yourself some time to forget, you'll be able to pick up on any strange changes in tone and re-paint them.

Many writers go awry with tense, especially when switching back and forth from a flashback. It's also a little confusing to keep things untangled when you're writing things that are happening in your mind. But these things aren't actually happening in real life– you're making them up as you go along. At the same time you're describing them as if they're already happened, because you know how it ends. But at the end of the day, you have to write it for a reader who's following each step.

Yeah. It's really that confusing, when you lay it all out.

Essentially, with all of the different points of view involved– yours as the writer, the character, and the reader– it's easy to get confused and write something like, "He threw the car keys at Maria and walks up the stairs to the apartment." No, he didn't doesn't. That's not how verbs work, so it's important to keep your tenses consistent. Observe carefully when your characters are "doing" versus "done" so that your reader doesn't have to take a time machine to get through your story.

And lastly, try not to waver between perspectives unless you are deliberately changing the point of view. With all respect to Mr. Faulkner, it's difficult on the reader and the writer to understand what's happening. It's perfectly fine to write one chapter from one character's perspective and then shift to another character's perspective as long as the reader is aware. Think back to the "Wheel of Perspective" exercise for practice in maintaining a steady point of view.

Consistency is how we, as writers, keep it real. And, by following both of these tips in conjunction, you'll find it easier to maintain consistency in all elements of your writing.

And when you have a consistent, descriptive, entertaining, immersive, informative, and compelling story, that's when you know you've finished writing your first fiction piece.

Conclusion

"Alright," said Mama Bear, clapping her hands. "We've reached the end of the book. What did my little bears learn?"

"I learned how to create relatable characters," cried Benny Bear excitedly, grabbing his small yellow hat before it leapt from his full head of curly chestnut hair.

Not to be outdone, Betty Bear stood up and fairly shouted, "I know how to write dynamic dialogue!" She jumped as she spoke, waving her hands.

From the darkest corner of the room, the shy voice of Bartholomew Bear could almost be heard. "I'm going to pay more attention to my story's setting. I didn't realize the time and place could be so important."

And Barbara Bear jumped onto her mother's lap, wrapping her arms around her neck and giving her a big sloppy kiss on the cheek before confiding in a very serious tone, "I didn't realize how much I'd been focusing on the plot. Thank you for teaching us, Mama Bear."

"It's been my pleasure," Mama Bear replied kindly. "Now, what will my little bears do if they find themselves stuck at any time?"

The little bears looked at each other. Benny met eyes with Betty, and Bartholomew stepped out of the shadows. Together they cried in one voice, "Just keep writing!"

I hope you've enjoyed our lessons together. It wasn't until I started writing this book that I realized how difficult the task at hand would become. Writers are artists, and just as I wouldn't tell Monet how to paint water lilies, or encourage Michaelangelo to try something not so religious, I don't want to stifle you or force you to do something "just like this".

As a result, this book is light on procedure and heavy on recommendations and concepts. I want to encourage you to write, keep writing, and then write some more, which is why I've shared several exercises with you. If you find yourself staring at a blank page, try one of these exercises to help you get back on track. Whether you write about the characters who are eluding you at the moment, or find some new imaginary people to play with, doing writing exercises is one of my favorite ways to get my head in the game. But if it doesn't work today, be patient with yourself, and remember that you are not a writing machine.

You are a writer. A good writer. You are writing a story, and that's not easy.

Now go forth and start planning. I can't wait to read what you've written someday!

If you're interested in learning to write books, chances are high that you've tried before and gotten stuck. As a result, you may be even less enthusiastic about trying again. If that's the case, check out some personally selected writing exercises from author Lauren Bingham's vault of helpful tricks and tips for getting the cursor moving again... or for the first time.

Go to

to download your own copy of Lauren Bingham's Five Favorite Writing Exercises.

REVIEWS

Reviews and feedback help improve this book and the author. If you enjoy this book, we would greatly appreciate it if you could take a few moments to share your opinion and post a review on Amazon.

Made in United States
North Haven, CT
31 January 2025

65197714R00163